An Author's Research Notes on Medieval England

~ A Guide for Aspiring Writers of Historical Fiction

By TL Clark

Published in the United Kingdom by:

Steamy Kettle Publishing

First published in electronic format and in print in 2025.

Text copyright © 2025 TL Clark

All rights reserved. No portion of this book may be reproduced, stored in a retrieval system or transmitted at any time or by any means mechanical, electronic, photocopying, recording, or otherwise without prior written permission of the publisher.

The right of TL Clark to be identified as the author of this work has been asserted by her in accordance with the Copyright, Designs and Patents Act 1988.

To the best of the author's knowledge, all facts are correct at the time of publishing.

This book was written by a human. No Artificial Intelligence (AI) has been used in the production of this book.

ISBN: 978-1-0682853-0-1

Acknowledgements

Cover design by Paul Trevena, with many thanks.

My gratitude to my husband, as always – my number one fan and the guy who ensures I'm fed and caffeinated even in my deepest writing state.

My editor, alpha, beta and proof readers have my undying appreciation.

And thank you, dear reader, for choosing this book.
May it assist you on your exciting writing path.

Dedication

This book is dedicated to intrepid explorers of history, which now includes you.

To study the past so we may avoid repeating mistakes is my wish for humanity.
But just doing so for fun or writing is a very good place to start.

To all writers, past, present and future,
If each of us were a single stitch,
Together we'd make a beautiful tapestry.
We are all important.
Write your story – be part of this wondrous world of literature.

Table of Contents

Chapter   Page No.

MEDIEVAL OVERVIEW

MEDIEVAL ERA DEFINITION	1
THE PERIODS OF MEDIEVAL ENGLAND	3
GREAT BRITAIN VS THE UK	4
MONARCHS OF MEDIEVAL ENGLAND	9
SOCIETY IN MEDIEVAL ENGLAND	15
RELIGION OF MEDIEVAL ENGLAND	25
MAJOR EVENTS IN MEDIEVAL ENGLAND	29
THE POLITICS OF MEDIEVAL ENGLAND	43
WEATHER OF MEDIEVAL ENGLAND	47
LOCATION (Cities, Towns and Villages)	49

15th CENTURY DETAILS

INTRODUCTION TO THE 15th CENTURY	61
NAMES	65
WHO'S IN CHARGE?	71
HOUSING	81
FOOD OF 15th CENTURY ENGLAND	97
FARMING	133
WILDLIFE	147
MEDICINE AND DISEASE	151
HYGIENE AND BEAUTY	183
FEMININE HYGIENE & CHILDBIRTH	193
RELIGION	209
TELLING THE TIME	243
MONEY	253
SERVANTS	259
WRITING	267
EDUCATION	279
LAW	291
CLOTHING / FASHION	305
KNIGHTS AND WEAPONRY	325
TRANSPORT	343
PASTTIMES	353
INSULTS / SLANG	367
FAVOURITE RESOURCES	377

Important Introduction

This book contains information that I, the author, TL Clark, gathered whilst conducting research for my medieval fiction books. Everything has been cross-referenced across more than one source. However, history is only ever the interpretation of the person viewing it.

One always seeks documentary evidence, but again, even that is written from one person's perspective. We each of us view life through the lens of our own lived experience.
e.g. For many a year, we were led to believe that Richard III was a "hunchback", thanks in part to William Shakespeare. But when the king's body was dug up (yes, from underneath a car park!), it was discovered that this was not the case – there may have been a slight twist to his spine indicating scoliosis, but not a forward bend. It would hardly be noticeable at all when clothed.
Therefore, historical FACTS are often a difficult beast to pin down. Perhaps, opinions of history which meet a popular consensus are as close as we may get. So, if you find yourself disagreeing with any of the contents, please feel free to do so, but in a respectful way. Just know that this is the best information I could personally gather and am sharing it out of the goodness of my heart.

During the course of this book, you will learn a lot of information. But you do not have to include all of it in your book. In fact, I urge you not to. Because the 'info dump' in books is a tedious thing.
Give detail only when/where the story requires it. Some things are pertinent to the plot, others are not.
e.g. We do not need to know the *maker* of an item of furniture, or even really the material of the item, but your characters may need to sit on a stool/chair/bench, and it's good to know which they were likely to perch upon.

A lot of research is for the author's info only. You know the ins and outs of the past so you can give an essence of it to your readers.

In the second half of this book, which goes into detail, I have included some little chapter header images. These were drawn by my own fair hands. I am not an artist (clearly!). These are for amusement more than accuracy, and because my own eyes can't cope with too much text without variation.
This is also the section where you will find some writing prompts a) for fun and b) to get your brain ticking.

NB I do use the terms BC and AD – I'm of an age where that is what I was taught, and my neurodivergent brain gets confused between BCE and CE. I imply no religious bias or offence by this. It's just what makes sense to me.

This Book's Mission Statement

So, look, to write *Love in the Roses* and *Love Habit*, I did a **lot** of research. Having spent hours upon hours (3 years total, including writing time) trawling The Internet and rifling through books, I collated a whole heap of notes. I cross-referenced information as I went, trying to ensure everything I'd gathered was as accurate as I could possibly make it.

If you read *How To Write A Historical Novel And Love It*, also by me, you will be familiar with the, **"When, what, why, where, who,"** method of research that I recommend. But please don't worry if you've not read it yet; it's not a prerequisite. That book handles the high-level approach to researching, writing, formatting, publishing and advertising a historical book. It poses thought-provoking questions and prompts to help you get started.

This book, however, is a companion to that, and is a collection of all my lovely research notes. Its purpose is to offer other authors (presumably, like yourself) an easy one-stop-shop to at least get the bulk of what you'll need to know before embarking upon your own wonderful tale. So that you can create realistic works of fiction.

Whether you're writing a historical fiction, romance novel or even a fantasy one, I hope you find information herein which helps give colour and shape to your story.

There will probably still be stuff you want/need to check for yourself. I don't know the details of what you're writing – there are always specifics. But, as I just said, it's a good starting point.

I've tried to lay it out in some semblance of order in a way that's easy to digest.

There is:
- a section giving an overview of the entire medieval era
- and then a more detailed section about 15th-century England

It's also scattered with my British wit, because nobody wants a boring book, do they? And hey, I just can't help the snark.

Anyway, this book is my way of helping other authors and is offered with loving kindness.

MEDIEVAL OVERVIEW

MEDIEVAL ERA DEFINITION

Righty-ho, we'll begin with the basics. The medieval era, aka mediaeval period or the Middle Ages – that's what we're looking at in this book, obviously.

Fun fact: until the nineteenth century, 'Middle Ages' was the term which was used.

Some historians then used the Latin "medium ævum" - 'medium' meaning the middle and 'aevum' meaning age. Around 1817, this was contracted to mediæval. Then, in 1876, another historian's book changed that to "medieval". Typewriters don't have an 'æ' key, so a choice had to be made. The British seemed to favour the 'ae' whilst Americans appeared to prefer to drop the 'a'. By the mid-twentieth century, most people seemed to adopt the "medieval" spelling.

So, **Middle Ages/mediæval/mediaeval/medieval** – it's all the same and all are acceptable. And I reserve the right to use them interchangeably.

Anyway...
The time *before* the Middle Ages was Ancient Britain. And it was *followed by* Early Modern Britain (starting with the Tudors).

The Middle Ages themselves can be split into:
- ❖ Early Middle Ages (410 - 1066)
- ❖ High Middle Ages (1066 - 1272)
- ❖ Late Middle Ages (1272 - 1485)

Even these terms are subject to discussion btw.

But, as you can see, the era spans a very long time – around 1,000 years (*gulp*). Clearly, I'm not going to be able to tell you absolutely everything that happened. And my own research focused on the fifteenth century. But let's see what we can find to get you started.

THE PERIODS OF MEDIEVAL ENGLAND

- **Dark Ages** start: 410 AD
- **Anglo-Saxon** (raids & settlement) (fabled King Arthur lives here!): 449 – c550
- **Separate Anglo-Saxon Kingdoms**: c550 – 924
- **United Anglo-Saxon**: 924 – 1066 (Danish Rule: 1016 – 1042)
- **Norman Period**: 1066 – 1154 (The Anarchy: 1135 – 1148)
- **The Plantagenets** (ends with The Wars of the Roses): 1154 – 1485
  (The fictional Robin Hood would have lived around the beginning of the 13th century.)

We know that the century name sounds later than it is, right? So, for example, the 15th century is the 1400s. Just checking.

GREAT BRITAIN VS THE UK

The difference between GB and the UK is quite subtle, and even people who were born here get confused, so let's clear this up a bit.

In today's terms:
Great Britain is a **landmass**, containing the countries of England, Scotland and Wales (the mainland/island).

The **sovereign state** is actually named the United Kingdom of Great Britain and Northern Ireland. This is a bit of a mouthful, so it's usually just referred to as the **UK**.

The **countries** England, Northern Ireland, Scotland and Wales form the **UK** (at the time of writing, at least).

We then add something called the **British Isles**, which include all of Ireland, Great Britain, The Isle of Man, The Isles of Scilly, The Channel Islands (which are made up of Jersey, Guernsey, Alderney and Sark), and 6,000 smaller islands.

Phew! Still with me? No wonder we're all a bit confused, eh?

How this all evolved:
- It was the Romans who named us **Britannia**. A Latin term which may come from the Common Brittonic/Greek name for our island, *Pritanī*, which may have meant "the painted ones" or "the tattooed folk," in Gaulish. The people were the **Britons**.
- 927 – King Æthelstan unified various Anglo-Saxon kingdoms to form the **Kingdom of England**.
- Around 1066, the term **English** was used to describe the native population of England (distinguished from Normans and French occupiers). Long before that, *Englisc* had been used, meaning "of the Angles".
- 1474 – Britain became great because of the French - they used *Bretagne* for both Britain (the country) and Brittany (in France), so clarification was needed. Ergo **Great Britain** was the name given to our nation.
- **Wales** (a conglomeration of Celtic kingdoms) was formally united with England by the Acts of Union of 1536 and 1542.
- In 1603, King James VI of Scotland also became King of England and King of Ireland. This was the **Union of the Crowns.** He **titled himself King of Great Britain**. But it was a personal (or dynastic) union only. For each crown maintained its own separate state; England, Ireland and Scotland merely shared a monarch who directed domestic and foreign policies for them.
- The two separate places. the Kingdom of England and the Kingdom of Scotland, united under the **Act of Union in 1707**, when we first officially became a state; the **Kingdom of Great Britain**. "United into One Kingdom by the Name of Great Britain". Queen Anne was on the throne. Yay, a woman was

our first joint ruler! And we, her peoples finally became **British**. The term British had been kicking around before but seems to have been used more for the Welsh and Cornish folk.
- In 1800, a further Act of Union brought **Ireland** formally into GB (but had sort of been under English control since the 1600s).
- **The Republic of Ireland** gained independence in 1922, comprising 26 of the 32 counties of Ireland, located in the southern part of the island. But six of Ulster's nine counties remained part of the United Kingdom as **Northern Ireland**.

This long history of Britannia, Britons, Great Britain etc. is probably why we like the abbreviation of 'Brits' – it encompasses it all.

By the way, the flag of the UK is the **union flag** (the red, white and blue cross). It only becomes the Union Jack when it's on board a Royal Navy ship (flown from the jackstaff).

The Flag of the Kingdom of Great Britain was created by James VI of Scotland aka James I of England – given he united the two kingdoms, it shouldn't be a huge surprise to learn he created the flag out of the two; the blue & white St Andrew's Cross of Scotland and the white & red St George's Cross of England. Apologies to the Welsh; you were believed to be part of England at the time so were represented with the St George's element. But how cool would it be to now add a dragon?

However, during the Act of Union in 1707, the white & red cross of Saint Patrick (which sits along the diagonals) was added to create the full Union Flag we know today.

Whilst we're discussing flags, the **St George's Cross**, as stated, is the red cross on a white background. And it has an interesting history.

St George supposedly flew this flag at the Battle of Antioch in 1098. English (and French) Crusaders then used this flag in 1188. The very word "crusade" comes from *crux*; Latin for cross.

King Edward I's troops are said to have displayed this emblem around 1270, which seems to have been when England *began* to adopt it as our own.

But there were others, such as the **Royal Banner**. In a book of all flags in 1367, England is represented by a plain red one. After the Reformation of the 1530s, St George's was the only saints banner, or indeed any religious flag, permitted to be flown in England – apparently, even Henry VIII had respect for it.

Whilst St George is the patron saint of England, he probably never visited here. He was born in where we now call Turkey, became a warrior for Rome and died a martyr in Palestine – no dragons were harmed (probably).

So, although we now view it as the flag of England, it sort of wasn't for a long time. Sorry.

That's a whole load of info. My apologies. So...

What all this means for the medieval writer:
Basically, in the medieval era, we had **kings and queens of *England* only** (with the others having their own leader). Its inhabitants were English.

We had separate *kingdoms*.
Who the *first king of England* was is a subject of debate.

Offa of Mercia and Egbert of Wessex ruled large parts following Roman rule (who themselves were here much longer than I appreciated at school, by the way). But majority is not all.

I used to think of Alfred the Great (born 849 AD) as the first king, but using the same approach as above, he was King of Wessex only. Sorry, Alfred.

Æthelstan is now commonly regarded as the first King of England from 927 (King of Anglo-Saxons from 924).

But if you want to get super sniffy, William I in 1066 brought in the Anglo-Norman era and *could* claim the honour of being our first king. Especially as the regnal numbers began with him - but they only kick in if another monarch comes along with the same name afterwards, and there was only one Æthelstan. I guess it depends on your own heritage and beliefs (*shrug*).

This seems like a good time to look at our monarchs.

MONARCHS OF MEDIEVAL ENGLAND

Let us look at the kings (and queens) of medieval England. Each monarch leaves their mark on the country (whether that's a shiny sheen or a dirty smear, I shall leave up to your discretion). Their rule holds many tales and narratives. But look, this isn't a 'history of kings and queens' book. I'll list them, but it's up to you to seek out all the gritty details if you need to. Otherwise, this book will go on forever.

I'll start from Alfred the Great in case you consider him the first one.

House of Wessex (886 – 1013)

- Alfred the Great: 886 – 899 (King of the Angles and Saxons)
- Edward the Elder: 899 – 924
- Ælfweard: 924 (for a couple of weeks and uncrowned)
- **Æthelstan the Glorious: 924 – 939 (King of Wessex and first King of England)**
- Edmund the Magnificent: 939 – 946
- Eadred: 946 – 955
- Eadwig All-Fair: 955 – 959
- Edgar the Peaceful: 959 – 975
- Edward the Martyr: 975 – 978
- Æthelred the Unready: 978 – 1013

House of Denmark (1013 – 1014)

- Sweyn Forkbeard: 1013 – 1014

House of Wessex – Restored (1014 – 1016)

- Æthelred the Unready (again): 1014 – 1016
- Edmund Ironside: 1016 (Apr-Nov)

House of Denmark – Restored (1016 – 1042)

- Cnut the Great (careful how you spell that!): 1016 – 1035
- Harold Harefoot: 1035 – 1040
- Harthacnut: 1040 – 1042

House of Wessex – Restored Again! (1042 – 1066)

- Edward the Confessor: 1042 – 1066

House of Godwin (1066)

- Harold II / Harold Godwinson: 1066 (Jan-Oct)

Anyone know what happened in 1066? Ah, The Battle of Hastings. A huge moment in England's rich tapestry (see what I did there? Any fans of the Bayeux here? *Awkward cough* Moving on…).

House of Wessex – Well, sort of but not really (1066)

Edgar Ætheling was *nominated* king but never ruled. The Normans wouldn't have it, so he submitted to…

House of Normandy (1066–1135)

- **William I** / William the Conqueror (aka William the Bastard): 1066 – 1087 (first Norman king)
- William II / William Rufus: 1087 – 1100
- Henry I / Henry Beauclerc: 1100 – 1135

House of Blois (1135–1154)

- Stephen of Blois: 1135 – 1154

Now, Henry I had supposedly declared Matilda heir presumptive, which the barons acknowledged. However, her cousin, Stephen of Blois (above), seized the throne. Insert anarchy here! I'm going to list her as a queen. She was sort of the first woman to get the role, even if she was never actually crowned. Hmph!

- Empress Matilda: 1141 (Apr-Nov) (not crowned)

House of Plantagenet (1154–1485)

When Stephen of Blois took back his throne, it was via the Treaty of Wallingford. In that treaty, he accepted the son of Matilda and Geoffrey V of Anjou (also named Henry) as the designated heir. So…

- Henry II / Henry Curtmantle: 1154 – 1189
- Richard I / Richard the Lionheart: 1189 – 1199
- John Lackland: 1199 – 1216

Louis the Lion (was never crowned, but he was proclaimed king in St Paul's Cathedral). He suffered a military defeat and was paid handsomely to surrender his right to become a legitimate king. Dodgy dealings!

- ❖ Louis the Lion: 1216 – 1217 (but not officially)

The crown then reverted to John's line.

- ❖ Henry III / Henry of Winchester: 1216 – 1272
- ❖ Edward I / Edward Longshanks: 1272 – 1307 (all of Henry VIII's wives could trace their heritage back to this guy. He's a pretty key figure.)
- ❖ Edward II / Edward of Caernarfon: 1307 – 1327 (abdicated then murdered)
- ❖ Edward III / Edward of Windsor: 1327 – 1377
- ❖ Richard II / Richard of Bordeaux: 1377 – 1399

Edward III's third surviving son, John of Gaunt (1st Duke of Lancaster) had a son; another Henry. He then seized power…

House of Lancaster

- ❖ Henry IV / Henry of Bolingbroke: 1399 – 1413 (usurper)
- ❖ Henry V / Henry of Monmouth: 1413 – 1422

Then we arrive at The Wars of the Roses (1455 – 1485). There's a bit of to and fro between the houses of Lancaster and York here, but they're both Plantagenet – futile!

- Henry VI (Lancaster): 1422-1461
- Edward IV (York): 1461-1470
- Henry VI (again): 1470-1471 (imprisoned & died)
- Edward IV (again): 1471-1483 (died)
- Edward V: Apr-Jun 1483 (not crowned & mysteriously disappeared along with his brother, aka The Princes in the Tower)
- Richard III (York): 1483-1485

Richard III then died at the Battle of Bosworth, where Henry Tudor was crowned, thus **ending the medieval era**. His mother was a great-granddaughter of John of Gaunt. And he represented the house of Lancaster. To be honest, his claim to the throne was a bit flimsy, but it was greatly strengthened by his marriage to Elizabeth of York (the red rose of Lancaster and the white rose of York were then joined to create the Tudor Rose).

House of Tudor (1485 – 1603)

- Henry VII (Tudor): 1485-1509

SOCIETY IN MEDIEVAL ENGLAND

To begin to get a better understanding of what life was like, we need to understand who was in charge. I'm going to try to keep this simple. If we go from the 6th century, Catholicism was the main religion. But be careful; there are periods of different religions (see the section on religion to follow).

But, whilst the Roman Catholic church was in control, the **hierarchy of power** generally looked like this:

- Pope
- Monarch
- Nobles
- Knights/Vassals
- Merchants/Farmers/Craftsmen
- Peasants/Serfs

Ranks of Nobility

Within the class of noblemen/nobles, you had the following groups:

- King
- Duke
- Marquess
- Earl
- Viscount
- Baron

But it depends whenabouts you're writing. It changed over time. So, a little detail on the evolution of this, in chronological order.

Earls are a bit complicated, as originally there was the Anglo-Saxon term of *ealdordom* - from the end of the 9th century, it was a term used to denote leaders of shires. This became *'eorl'* in the 11th century. The first 'earls', or at least earldoms, seem to have been brought into existence in 1017.

William I entrusted lands to his **barons** in 1066. Said barons formed the Royal Council which would meet with the king when summoned. This was what formed the foundations of what became the House of Lords as we know it today. The barons' lands were passed down to their descendants via primogeniture. There were only ever around twenty-five barons at any given time.

The first **duke** was created by Edward III in 1337. The maximum number of dukes in England has only ever reached 500. Currently, the total stands at 24.

The title of **marquess** came into being in 1385, thanks to Richard II.

Henry VI created the first **viscount** in 1440.

These make up the titles in the peerage. In medieval England, these titles inferred military might.

Knights, by the way, have never been part of the peerage. However, they were greatly respected. And in the medieval era, they were most definitely military.

Knights first appeared around the 8th century. It was *not* a hereditary title. One had to earn it. But it was cost-prohibitive. The training wasn't cheap. And the cost of the armour was horrendous; the 'off the peg' style would (in today's money) set you back around £22,000 (around $30,000), but a full set of plate armour, made to measure in the 15th century, could cost around £1million! I've seen other costs put at around £6,000-11,000. But you get my drift; it was expensive.

Although the title itself didn't pass down, knights often expected their sons to follow suit. The Code of Chivalry was developed in the 11th-12th centuries to temper the rather thuggish/lout behaviour amongst knights.

But be careful if you're writing about knights. They're not necessarily what stories and movies have shown them to be. And, actually, by the Battle of Bosworth in 1485 (one of the concluding battles of the Wars of the Roses), Henry VII is said to have brought 5,000 men with him, 1,800 of whom were mercenaries.

Between 1358-1488, there were 68 **women** conferred with the honour of knight, by the way.

Forms of Address

It's always important to address people correctly. Again, this changes through time, but as a rule of thumb during the medieval period:

- **King** – Your Grace
- **Duke** – Your Grace (by inferiors)
  Very close friends may just use the name associated with his title, e.g. Hesford (for the Duke of Hesford)
  & his wife: Your Grace / Madam / Duchess (title)
- **Marquess** – My Lord / My Lord Marquess / Lord (title)
  & his wife: Madam / Lady (title)
- **Earl** – My Lord / Lord (title)
  & his wife: Madam / Lady (title)
- **Viscount** – My Lord / Lord (title)
  & his wife: Madam / Lady (title)
- **Baron** – Lord (title)
  & his wife: Madam / Lady (title)
- **Knight** – Sir (first name)
  & his wife: Lady (surname)
- **Bishop** – Your Excellency
- **Priest** – Sir (first name)

If in doubt, 'my lord' was often a safe bet when addressing someone you suspected of being your superior. Who can go wrong with a, "Yes, my lord"? Anyone below the status of prince would accept this. Sire also seems to have been acceptable.

For the female nobles, 'my lady' was fairly universal.

When addressing someone you know to be your direct superior, 'my liege' *may* be suitable. e.g. a peasant speaking to his landowner noble/knight, or that noble when addressing the king may use 'my liege'. But beware; this was not commonly used and infers 'my liege lord' in the feudal sense – the one you're pledged to.

Only if you use 'sir' before a name does it need to be capitalised, e.g. Sir William.

If one is speaking to someone of a lower order, one could use their first name.

The matter of names can become quite complex tbh. It rather depends on the relationship one has with whom one is conversing, or indeed, whether it is in correspondence. So as not to fill an entire book with all the who's, what's and wherefore's, I shall direct you towards the website **https://www.chinet.com/~laura/html/titles12.html** which has many many pages on all the details and a helpful chart.

Fun fact: Consensus of opinion is that Henry VIII was the first King of England to be called "Your Majesty". Again, debatable.

But how did all of this power trickle down into daily life?

Feudalism

~ *The relationship between the monarch and his nobles; political and military*

Feudalism was the social system in which the Crown allowed the nobility to hold lands in exchange for service (land tenure), particularly but not exclusively military service, during the 9th - 15th centuries. Allegedly, William the Conqueror brought Anglo-Norman feudalism in.

The lands were known as fiefdoms or fiefs (pronounced feef or /fiːf/, y'know, like a Londoner saying thief).

The monarch still *owned* the lands. The landholders were referred to as vassals (/ˈvas(ə)l/). They were rich folk (aristocrats), usually in the form of barons or knights. The tenant-in-chief.

The people who sublet these fiefs were called mesne-tenants (meen or /mēn/). *Mesne* being Anglo-French for intermediate/intervening.

Solemn oaths of homage (hommidge or /ˈhɒm.ɪdʒ/) and fealty had to be sworn to become a vassal, whereby they would pledge to offer military protection.

Does that make sense? The nobles basically rented their lands from the monarch as long as they promised to fight for him when called upon.

NB It is now widely debated whether feudalism actually existed. However, I'm still including it here as the debate continues.

Manorialism

~ The relationship between a noble and his peasants; economic and social

Manorialism was a part of the feudal system in the rural economy. It was at its height around the 11th to 15th centuries.

The lord of the manor was granted legal and economic powers to oversee a fief. He lived in the manor house.

The **villein** (the type of peasant who worked this way) then lived on and worked the land for their lord, often three days per week. They were each assigned a plot of land to grow vegetables for their own food, so would farm that when not working directly for the manorial estate, so it's not like they were resting on their 'days off'.

Serfs, ergo, were similar to villeins, but were considered the property of the lord, not permitted to leave his lands, and given no remuneration for their labour.

Whereas villeins could leave should the need arise, as long as they had permission from their lord. Both could befall harsh treatment by the landholder, although he was supposed to offer protection. Villeins had slightly more legal rights, though. And serfs would be expected to work more days.

Once the villein died, there were no inheritance rights. So, any descendants would have to seek to renew the lease with the lord.

Education was deemed of little importance, and so the majority of peasants were pretty much illiterate (more on that later, in the education section). Children would help their parents work as soon as they were able.

It was possible for villeins to learn a trade and become a craftsman.

During the early part of the Middle Ages, workers would make payments in grain, eggs etc. (crops and livestock) to their lord (via the bailiff). But this slowly changed.

Particularly, after the Black Death (more on that later), the population decreased dramatically, which led to a labour shortage. And the economy slowly turned towards a monetized one (mercantilism), which reached its peak in the 17th century.

Guilds

All throughout the Middle Ages, guilds had formed; organisations. They fell into two categories: merchant and craft.

The **merchant guilds** dealt with international affairs, as that's where their trade led them. These were the money and policy men who held influence over local government.

Whereas **craft guilds** were more like your small business groups. They represented occupations, e.g. bakers, blacksmiths, butchers, fishmongers, fletchers, goldsmiths, grocers, shipwrights and tailors.

They also participated in religious services. Most prominently, on main feast days, they would have provided pageants in grand processions. Each craft had a play to represent their skill, e.g. the shipwrights created pageants of Noah's Ark. Elaborate scenes and costumes had to be provided, often on moving carts. And there was great competition and rivalry between each guild.

Folk all clubbed together in their guilds to increase and protect their income, essentially. Whilst also being as pious as possible to avoid purgatory.

Burghers

Nom, nom, nom. OK, not that kind of burger, but it does sound the same.

Somewhere between the serfs and the nobles, arose a new class. Earlier in the Middle Ages, they were viewed as a subclass of peasant. However, they climbed up the ranks to create their own section of society.

They were business owners, merchants and other generally wealthy people — a result of industry and commerce. The important thing is that they were **citizens** of a particular town. Therefore, they were either born into a citizen family or resided in the city for a determined number of years whilst engaging in respectable business and had the recommendation of an existing citizen. Of course, there was a fee involved.

So, not all inhabitants were citizens. And not all citizens were burghers. Only the most prosperous and prestigious folk reached that status. Therefore, they took a keen interest in the politics of their area and held influence.

Fun fact: Burgher is where we get the term bourgeoisie; a derogatory term for middle-class folk who are materialistic.

RELIGION OF MEDIEVAL ENGLAND

From around 476, Catholicism held supreme power in Europe. However, England has always been a bit of an odd duck.

After the departure of the (Catholic) Romans, Germanic settlers brought paganism into the country in the 5th century. Although, pockets of Catholic communities remained.

It wasn't until the late 6th and early 7th centuries that the people returned to Christianity (Catholicism). In 597, Augustine became the first archbishop of Canterbury (the first monastery in the country), and King Æthelberht converted to Christianity.

In 627, King Edwin of Northumbria (north of England), was baptized, along with his nobles. However, after his death in 632, most of his people reverted to paganism.

In 630, the King of East Anglia (east of England), sought the help of the archbishop of Canterbury to help convert his people. Also, around that time, the West Saxons (roughly, the Hampshire region) adopted Christianity as their faith.

And in 653, King Penda of Mercia (Midlands) was baptized. Lastly, Sussex converted in 681 under King Æðelwealh with the aid of St Wilfrid.

However, the Danes in the 9th century brought a further resurgence of paganism when they conquered most of England. Their raids destroyed many religious buildings.

But Alfred the Great, King of Wessex, was victorious over the Danes in battle in 878. He made a treaty with them, and they agreed to become Christian.

Oh, but there was yet another plot twist. The Normans (from 1066) embraced parts of the Anglo-Saxon religion.

Saint Dunstan (archbishop of Canterbury) reformed the monasteries in late 10th century. And Catholicism grew even further, with many new churches and monasteries being built.

King John, who did much wrong, fell foul of Pope Innocent III as he wanted to appoint Stephen Langton archbishop of Canterbury. The king did not. The Pope eventually placed England under papal interdict (effectively excommunicating the entire country) from 23 March 1208 – 02 July 1214. Churches were closed.

At which point, King John surrendered England to the papacy in 1213, making it a Papal fief – paying an annual tribute to His Holiness. This did give England papal protection, but at a high cost. And Langton became archbishop of Canterbury.

Not until 1365, did Parliament manage to declare that surrender invalid. England threw off the yoke of being a papal state and became an independent kingdom.

So, by the 13th century, after much toing and froing, Christianity (Catholicism) became the main religion of England. Bishops ruled over their dioceses from their palaces.

But… the Protestants were coming! In 1516, Martin Luther, a German theologian, wrote his "95 Theses - disputations on indulgences". And, in 1525, William Tyndale translated the New Testament from Latin into English. The Protestants didn't hold much sway until Henry VIII sulked and established the Church of England after the medieval era.

Phew! What a tumultuous time. You get what I mean when I say it's complicated? So, just double check which year you're writing about, and ensure you get the main religion right.

MAJOR EVENTS IN MEDIEVAL ENGLAND

There are times in life that have more of an impact than others. Some don't even seem that big at the time. Let's take a look at some key moments in the Middle Ages.

1066 - Battle of Hastings

As I have already mentioned, 1066 was when William I / The Conqueror invaded. It really was a pivotal moment in English history. An unassuming hill near Hastings in the south of England changed our way of life.

I won't repeat the information, but Anglo-Norman feudalism began here. Our society was given a new structure, and churches flourished. And **the Domesday Book** was completed under William's instruction. This Great Survey itself was fundamental to the new governance – King William now learned how much every land in every shire was worth (& what was due to him) and the resources involved (*quiet mutterings of "What an accountant!"*).

The Crusades

The First Crusade was launched in 1095, beginning a series of religious wars which sought to reclaim The Holy Land from Islamic rule (to Christians). It was a bitter, bloody time. There were at least eight crusades, the last of those being in 1270.

In 1099, Christians captured Jerusalem and European pilgrims began to visit, but many were attacked and killed along the route as it passed through Muslim-controlled territories. Thus, the **Knights Templar** were established; a military order of monks given papal recognition in 1129 (but formed around 1119) – they offered protection to said travellers. They wore a white habit emblazoned with a red cross.

However, the Knights Templar became too powerful. From 1139, they were free from having to pay taxes, and established a network of banks – their financial power grew. As too did their military might – they became fearsome warriors, defending the Crusader states of the Holy Land.

Eventually, they lost their foothold in the Holy Land, and established themselves instead in Paris. But proceeded to upset King Philip IV of France by denying him additional loans. By means of arrest, torture and burnings, the king brought down the order which was officially dissolved in 1312.

It could be argued that Europe remained Christian because of the Crusades, having slowed Islamic power.

For all the harm done (and there was a great deal of that), the crusaders did bring back medical knowledge and a new trade in spices. Silver linings? Eurgh.

University

Fun fact: (rather than a major event) – it is believed that Oxford University was founded in 1096; the first one in England. Coo lummy, that's an old institution! But more on old educational establishments later.

Thomas Becket aka Thomas à Becket

This chap was archbishop of Canterbury but was murdered in the cathedral on 29th December 1170. He had been a royal Chancellor beforehand, and a friend to King Henry II. However, they fell out big time. Thomas fled to France, but the Pope intervened, and King Henry assured him he'd be safe to return to England and retake his place as archbishop. But Thomas ruffled feathers again, excommunicating a few folk. The king was outraged and sent knights to kill the traitorous Thomas, who had only been put in the role so Henry could get his own way; ingrate! But Thomas actually grew a religious conscience whilst in situ.

Folk immediately proclaimed the now martyred man to have miraculous healing abilities. He was canonised on 21st February 1173 after more miracles occurred. A great shrine was erected in his name at Canterbury Cathedral, which became one of the most important sites of pilgrimage in Europe. His memory shone as a beacon against unbridled power and a defender of the Church.

Magna Carta

This magnificent document was signed on 15th June 1215. King John was a terrible terrible king. He was so bad that his barons held a rebellion. This 'Great Charter' was their way of limiting royal authority. Forever. This is what gave birth to our democracy. It established things such as the protection of individual rights and due process. A momentous piece of paper which is perhaps the finest example of the pen being mightier than the sword. Huzzah!

Parliament

The first parliament was called on 20th January 1265 by Simon de Montfort. Basically, Henry III had reneged on some provisions, which led to the Battle of Lewes in 1264 (Simon won!). He was effectively England's ruler for the next twelve months. This parliament stripped the king of unlimited authority. Simon insisted that representatives be *elected* not appointed. Democracy in practice started here.

(You can read more about parliament in the 'politics' section)

The Hundred Years War

It all started in April 1337. France vs England. Philip VI of France seized Aquitaine (previously held by the English). So, Edward III fought back, declaring himself the rightful King of France.

Much conflict ensued which saw new military tactics being utilised. Five generations carried on this feud, roping in allies from across Europe. The ending is a few entries below, but it all got seriously bloody.

The Black Death, 1348 - 1352

Also known as the bubonic plague, it changed England and much of Europe in 1348. Contemporary records referred to it as **the Great Pestilence** (The Black Death was a 19th century term which got applied).

It wiped out somewhere between 30-50% of the population of England. Yep, **around half the people in the country died!** And about a third of the European population. That's around 30 million people in total.

Not everybody who contracted the disease died (*tiny yay*), but about two-thirds of them did (*big boo*).

It was a terrible illness in every sense of the word. It started with incredibly sore buboes (red, swollen lymph nodes usually in the groin and armpits), which could turn black (hence the name). A high fever, headaches, vomiting and ataxia (loss of control over bodily movement) could accompany this. An increased tendency to bruise and bleed (including internal haemorrhaging) would follow. Lovely!? On the ^bright side^, it would often kill within 72 hours – quick and painful!

btw are we all familiar with the ^sarcastrophe^ ? It's the most awesome punctuation ever imho. Anyway....

I'm sorry, but the plague probably was spread by rats and their fleas. It wasn't even a new thing. The first records of a plague pandemic go back to around the 6th century. And likely originated in Asia, China specifically (they always seem to get the blame!). However, 1348 was when it first hit England.

It wasn't until the start of the 16th century that England's population got back to the level it had been in 1348 – around 200 years to repopulate!

Bubonic plague was a fairly regular occurrence during the medieval era (and beyond), with outbreaks in 1563, 1593, 1625 and 1665. The infamous Great Plague started in London in June 1665. The Great Fire of London in 1666 seemed to help reduce cases, but that could be coincidence. The sharp frosts that winter were possibly helpful. But I digress. We'll get to explore other ^fun^ diseases in the focused research section later – something to look forward to!

Other effects of the 1348 Black Death were far-reaching. Initially, wars and trade across Europe stopped. But only for a little while, because humans!

The more long-lasting consequence was the lack of labour. The **economic impact** was huge. Instead of services, landowners started charging tenants money rents. This did increase the mobility of the serfs, and people started to go to who paid them best. The squeeze on labour was still being felt in the 15th century (over one hundred years later). Ergo, it began the demise of serfdom. There was a rise in questioning authority, even of The Church! (*gasp*) and rebellion arose.

The Peasants' Revolt – 1381

The peasants are revolting! 15th June 1381, the Peasants Revolt was basically the workers trying to get better rights/working conditions.

It was also known as The Great Rising and Wat Tyler's Rebellion. It was the first major one of its kind in England (*punches air with fist*).

Many English people will cringe at the term 'poll tax' as it was a dastardly thing brought in by Maggie Thatcher in the 1990's. Now, if she'd looked at history a bit more closely, the riots of the 20th century would maybe have come as less of a surprise to her! Some might venture that they could've been avoided altogether.

Yes, the bad old poll tax was what sparked the populace to revolt in 1381.

As explained in the 'Black Death' section above, civil unrest had been steadily increasing since the plague. Well, most of your nearest and dearest dying painfully then the lack of food and loss of home would leave anyone a bit disgruntled! I mean, has anyone tried speaking to me without so much as a snacky-snack? This was a million times worse than that.

The Statute of Labourers (1351) tried to fix a *maximum* wage for labourers. Dude, don't kick people when they're down! Obviously, it upset people (*face palm*).

So, rebels from mostly Essex and Kent marched on London in May 1381, led by **Wat Tyler**. Flemish merchants got...there's no nice way to say it...they got massacred. And John of Gaunt's palace of the Savoy was razed (burned). **King Richard II** decided it was sensible to negotiate with these Essex men, and agreed to free trade, cheap land, and abolish serfdom and forced labour.

Meanwhile, the Kentish folk got The Tower of London to surrender! And the guys responsible for the poll tax, namely the chancellor, Archbishop Simon of Sudbury, and the treasurer, Sir Robert Hales, got their heads chopped off.

The mayor of London was so enraged that when he met Wat Tyler the next day, he reciprocated. In the king's presence! He then issued a loud, "Calm down!" (well, he reasoned with the rebels and got them to disperse by promising them reforms).

Rumblings of rebellion still continued in other counties for a couple of weeks. That is, until the bishop of Norwich stomped on the rebels of East Anglia at the end of June.

Of course, the king promptly forgot all about his promises, and the rebellion was a **failure**. However, there was no further levying of the poll tax. And I'm sure it acted as a cautionary tale (*cough*).

The Treaty of Windsor – 9th May 1386

Formed between England and Portugal, it is said to be the oldest surviving alliance in Europe. And was signed in Windsor, hence the name.

This also sealed the marriage between King John I of Portugal and Philippa of Lancaster – she was the daughter of John of Gaunt (mentioned as a bad guy in the Peasant's Revolt above). After winning a victory with the assistance of English archers, John I was recognised as the King of Portugal in a battle which ended the *interregnum* of the 1383–1385 Crisis.

Really, it all started back in 1147, when some English soldiers detoured on their way to the Crusades to help King Afonso Henriques conquer Lisbon, taking the city from the Moors.

England and Portugal have remained friends ever since – aww. Support and mutual understanding.

Battle of Agincourt, 25 October 1415

This was the decisive battle in **The Hundred Years War (1337–1453)**. Under King Henry V, the English gained victory over the French.

It had all begun when King Edward III of England decided he should also be the King of France, and invaded Flanders. There were many battles and toing and froing of who was in the lead.

There was a long period of truce, thanks to the French King Charles VI's daughter marrying King Richard II. However, Henry V had a massive ego and some authority issues, so tried to renew his claim to the French crown. Well, he'd usurped the English throne from Richard II, so why stop there? Tsk!

France had its own problems and was in a vulnerable position; King Charles VI was having psychotic episodes, and the French nobility had started squabbling for who was next in line. So, Henry thought it a marvellous opportunity. Of course, the French didn't agree, and a thrashing at Harfleur ensued.

Undeterred, the troops, having failed to cross the Somme River, ended up at Agincourt. The English numbers had dwindled, were exhausted from the long march, and dysentery was rife. Yet, somehow, despite being possibly outnumbered 5-1, they claimed victory. The battle lasted somewhere between thirty minutes and three hours, depending on who you asked – it was pretty quick!

Henry V indulged in full pomp and ceremony with parades in London, and *The Agincourt Carol* was written for him. And he sat comfortably on his throne.

Other famous battles during The Hundred Years War, where the English 'won' include:

- ❖ Battle of Crécy (1346)
- ❖ Battle of Poitiers (1356)

Henry managed to nab Normandy in 1419. And, with the Treaty of Troyes (1420), Henry V was declared heir to the French throne.

William Shakespeare then made sure nobody forgot all this by writing his play, aptly named, *Henry V*.

btw, years later, the French got their own back with the help of **Joan of Arc**, in the Siege of Orléans, 1429.

Wars of the Roses

Oh, look - more fighting. I mean, ffs, a ridiculously costly (in every sense) war had just ended! (*deep sigh and eyeroll*)

Known as **The Cousins War** at the time, the conflict began 22nd May 1455. For thirty years, battles broke out sporadically as the House of York challenged the House of Lancaster for the throne of England. They were all Plantagenets, so who really cared?? It led to political instability and a rather fraught period all round.

The key battles of these wars were:

- ❖ The Battle of St Albans (22 May 1455)
- ❖ The Battle of Northampton (10 July 1460)
- ❖ The Battle of Wakefield (30 December 1460)
- ❖ The Battle of Towton (29 March 1461)
- ❖ The Battle of Tewkesbury (4 May 1471)
- ❖ The Battle of Bosworth Field (22 August 1485) – which a lot of people call the last one as this is where Richard III died (on the battlefield; the last English king to do so)
- ❖ The Battle of Stoke Field (16 June 1487)

Henry VII (Tudor) won, and they all lived happily ever after (*cough*).

The Printing Press

A far nicer event. It's remarkable how much of a difference this made. Power to the people! The Church had controlled what we knew for ages. But now the common man was... (*insert dramatic music*)... learning!

The printing press was actually invented in China, possibly in the first millennium A.D., under the Tang Dynasty. By the 12th century, they'd made a moveable type (each block was a letter) and were producing books in great numbers.

In 1297, *Nung Shu* was printed – a treatise on agriculture and farming practises (riveting!). However, it is thought to be the first mass-produced book and found its way into Europe.

Johannes Gutenberg created the first printing press in Europe in 1450 – bit late to the party, but better late than never. This Gutenberg Press replaced wooden blocks with metal ones. And the *Gutenberg Bible* was the first book produced by this in 1452.

Italy, France, Spain and Portugal all caught on in the 1470s. As did England.

William Caxton (*cheers*) had been living in Bruges and studying in Cologne. He and Colard Mansion printed *The Recuyell of the Histories of Troye* (a French courtly romance) in Bruges, 1472 – **the first book printed in the English language**. Psst... *recuyell* means collection. Caxton was also still working as a diplomat, by the way. Busy busy busy!

In **1476**, William set up a printing press at Westminster, London – y'know where rich people lived who could afford books. Amongst the first books printed there was (the already verbally popular) *The Canterbury Tales* by Geoffery Chaucer – hurrah, now we're getting saucy!

Mr Caxton printed around 100 different books in his lifetime.

Now, this is the really good part. The Church had hitherto held a monopoly on book creation, and they wrote in Latin – because knowledge is power, and also it was understood universally (by those who needed to).

At this time, England had a great many dialects. It was possible to travel around the country and not understand your fellow countrymen. This may be why we have so many regional accents, but I digress.

William was originally from Kent but was now living in London. Londoners spoke in the dialect of the East Midlands, and that's what he used in his books. This became known as **Chancery Standard**, and heavily influenced Early Modern English. Basically, William Caxton made us speak standardised English. How cool is that?

Incidentally, Modern English is where we stopped using all grammatical gender – if you've ever learned a foreign language, you know how everything has to have a gender by way of a determiner e.g. the pen in French is *le stylo*. Or the swing in German becomes *die Schaukel*. Yeah, we just went with 'the', without gendering everything. This wasn't actually because of the printing press. It was a slow and steady parting of the ways, from around the 11th century.

I know I've wittered on a fair bit, but the printing press changed the lives and language of the English populace. And a fine event to end on.

THE POLITICS OF MEDIEVAL ENGLAND

Since the 10th century, there had been national councils or 'witans'. Church leaders and nobles (e.g. archbishops and barons) promoted legislation throughout the land and made decisions regarding war (and peace). So, it's not like there was nothing.

But, during the reign of Henry III in 1236, the meetings of 'the great council' became known as parliament (*hears a certain pirate call for parley; from the French for 'conversation'*). The meeting place was usually at Westminster.

On **20th January 1265**, Simon de Montfort called what is generally regarded as **the first true parliament**. This is when representation was established. Attendees included "burgesses" — elected officials from boroughs and towns which held burgage tenure, and knights.

These folk from different boroughs and counties now held *discussions and debates* on important matters (*three cheers for democracy!*). No longer was it just a way of spreading word of what the monarch commanded. The people had a say on the way they were governed, the laws decreed and (the always controversial) taxation levels.

NB Simon de Montfort had actually called a parliament in June 1264 to sanction this. But it's the 1265 one that's the biggie.

When Mr de Montford was killed at the Battle of Evesham in 1265, Henry III was restored. But parliament was here to stay.

Incidentally, the first *Parliament of the Kingdom of **Great Britain*** was established in 1707, following the merger of the Kingdom of England and the Kingdom of Scotland.

It then became the *Parliament of the **United Kingdom*** in 1801 - Ireland joined the United Kingdom via the Acts of Union 1800.

And it wasn't until after the Civil War during the 17th century that **political parties** were formed, namely **the Whigs** (liberal, reform types) and **the Tories** (monarchist, traditional aristocrats). Indeed, these evolved into the Liberal Democrats and the Conservatives we know in the UK today.

During the 14th century, two **Houses of Parliament** emerged. This is when the elected officials started to meet separately as the **House of Commons** aka the Lower House.

And the **House of Lords** or the Upper House – formed of the **Lords Spiritual** (the ecclesiastical chaps i.e. archbishops, bishops, abbots and sometimes even priors), and the **Lords Temporal** i.e. nobles/magnates (those with the rank of duke, marquess, earl, viscount or baron).

Over the course of the 15th century, those Lords Temporal became almost completely hereditary and became known as 'peers'.

So, that's the parliamentary aspect. But, of course, "political" can cover a broad context. I don't want to get too bogged down in the machinations for fear one shall get overly entangled and most writers won't need the nitty gritty detail of this stuff.

I can't cover the entire political history of the medieval era. There have always been opposing views, different sides of battles (figurative and literal) and family feuds. Social opinion status; 'It's complicated'.

The important thing to know is how England was governed. The monarch had the main control. But never underestimate the barons. Or the Church - after all, until Henry VIII, the monarchs all kind of answered to the Pope.

WEATHER OF MEDIEVAL ENGLAND

Two things to note:

- ❖ "Climactic optimum" / medieval warm period – 900-1300
- ❖ And the "Little Ice Ace" – started 14th century, peaked 1550-1700, ended around 1850

So, already, we can see that there was an unusually warm period (the summers during that time were about 1°C warmer and also drier than today), followed by a particularly cold one. These helped and hindered agriculture and therefore the economy respectively.

The 'Little Ice Age' was a time of weather phenomena such as sudden floods and snowstorms. As well as colder-than-normal winters.

However, for **general weather guidance**, based on data from the more modern times of 1910-2020 (as weather records didn't really start until then):

Month	Jan	Feb	Mar	Apr	May	Jun	Jul	Aug	Sep	Oct	Nov	Dec
Mean daily maximum °C	7	8	10	13	16	19	21	21	18	14	10	8
Mean daily minimum °C	2	2	3	4	7	10	12	12	10	7	4	2
Average precipitation days	13	11	10	10	10	10	10	11	10	13	14	14
Mean monthly sunshine hours	55	78	117	164	199	188	196	181	141	103	65	51

Table 1 – Historical weather data

Basically, the warmest months in England are May-September, with temperatures peaking in July.

The coldest months are December-March.

And the wettest months are, well, fairly evenly spread actually; this is England!

It's a good idea to check your specific year and region to see if there was any 'interesting weather' you might want to include.

Seasons

Now, I thought this was going to sound like me stating the bleedin' obvious. However, one of my recent social media posts suggests many people are confused. So, just to be clear, the UK seasons are considered to be:

- **Spring**: 20th March - 20th June
- **Summer**: 21st June – 23rd September
- **Autumn**: 24th September – 21st December
- **Winter**: 22nd December – 19th March

LOCATION (Cities, Towns and Villages)

Definitions:
- ❖ **City** - a large town. City status conferred by royal charter.
- ❖ **Town** - built around a market. Would have a borough charter, taxation as a town or summons of parliamentary representatives.
- ❖ **Village** - no market

Towns/Cities

These were built up, busy, over-crowded, dirty (due to horses and humans), hubs of commerce.

In the UK, city status may be given by the monarch, usually (but not necessarily) associated with a place having a cathedral (and/or, these days, a university). It's difficult to pin down how many actual cities there were back then, but there are currently 55 cities in England (plus 7 in Wales, 8 in Scotland and 6 in Northern Ireland).

Towns were usually owned by a lord. Market towns were increasingly popular due to the high levels of trade (in things such as food, clothing and household items) – this is where you would find most merchants and shops. But crime rates were high.

In 1086, a great survey of England was conducted, called the Domesday Book (actually, at the time its name was in Latin and translated as The Book of Winchester, but I digress). By its reckoning, there were over 100 boroughs (self-governing settlements/towns) at that time.

They were much smaller than our towns and cities of today. According to the first poll tax in 1377 we know that (in order of largest to smallest):

- London's population was 34,971 (as opposed to today's 9 million)
- York, the next biggest only had 10,872 inhabitants
- Bristol – 9,518
- Plymouth – 7,256
- Coventry – 7,226
- Norwich – 5,928
- Lincoln – 5,354
- Salisbury – 4,839
- King's Lynn – 4,691
- Colchester – 4,432
- Boston – 4,307
- Beverley – 3,994
- Newcastle – 3,970
- Canterbury – 3,861
- Bury St Edmunds – 3,668

I could go on, but you get the idea.

The total population in England in 1500 was around 3 million.

Incidentally, London seems to have always had the largest population. In the 15th century, the city had 12 main trades - clothworkers, drapers, fishmongers, goldsmiths, grocers, haberdashers, ironmongers, mercers, salters, skinners, tailors and vintners.

Also, there was a St Paul's Cathedral on Ludgate Hill. But the current one, designed by Sir Christopher Wren, was built 1675-1710.

Fun fact: Signs were hung outside shops with painted symbols of the shop's wares due to low levels of literacy. And you can sometimes still catch glimpses of these today.

Both **towns and cities often had walls**, or at least fences, surrounding them, to ensure some degree of protection. Entrance was via guarded gates. They were busy, crowded, noisy, dirty and smelly. There were no bin men - refuse piled up quickly! Sewage was also another issue.

Mop fairs took place in market towns, coinciding with quarter days (when rents would be collected). Serfs looking for new posts would gather, wearing a badge/emblem of their trade, offering themselves for hire.

Villages
Usually, villages would be no more than 8 miles away from a town.

Travel between these places was hard and perilous; bandits often roamed trade routes (see the "Transport' section for details). Also, language/dialect could differ greatly (see 'Language' under the 'Writing' section).

Countryside

Agriculture played a vital role, so was busy in a very different way.

For most of human history, the vast majority of folk would have been involved in one way or another in agriculture. The time before supermarkets was one of homegrown, seasonal produce. People would live in settlements, each supporting one another even indirectly e.g. tools supplied by the blacksmith were used in farming.

About 90% of the population lived in the countryside.

And around 60% of the labour force worked in agriculture itself (directly).

Some parts of the nation are very flat, some have rolling hills. There are lakes and coasts, caves and castles, valleys and cliffs. Do feel free to explore in your story.

The Capital City of England

London. London's the capital city, right? Right? Err...

Alfred the Great had made **Winchester** the capital of Wessex. Well, the court was mobile, so it wasn't quite a capital city as we know it to mean today. But it was very important.

King Athelstan held his council in **London**, and King Æthelred issued laws from there which increased its importance as a city.

William I (of 1066 fame) was crowned in the recently consecrated Westminster Abbey in London, and constructed the White Tower at the Tower of London as his home.

Parliament, formed in 1215, met in the Palace of Westminster. London thus became the political capital of the nation.

But Edward I moved the Chancery and Exchequer departments to **York** (1298 – 1304). So, during that time, York was technically the capital of England.

Oxford took its turn between 1644-1646. During the English Civil War, Charles I was expelled from London by Oliver Cromwell's Parliamentarian forces, and so he sought refuge in Christ Church, Oxford.

It wasn't until the Acts of Union in 1800 (which united the Kingdom of Great Britain and the Kingdom of Ireland to officially create the United Kingdom of Great Britain and Ireland) that the seat of the monarch was established as being at the Court of St. James, and a Parliament representing England, Scotland, Wales, and Ireland sitting in the Palace of Westminster, London. At that point, London became the de facto capital city of the UK.

But London's capital city status has never really been granted or confirmed by statute or in written form (*explodey brain emoji*).

British Place Names

I actually find place names fascinating but maybe that's a me thing. They give us massive clues about their history. And, if you're writing about nobility, you may want to invent a place name as their title/name e.g. Duke of Hesford.

So, how do the British get such weird place names? Well, it's all down to our mixed heritage....

The Celts
You'll find several rivers with 'Avon' in their title in the UK. That's because it's literally the Celtic word for river. The Welsh use 'Afon'.

But the towns the Celts named have 'Pen' in them e.g. Pendleton or Penrith – it means hill or headland. Or 'Coombe' (or 'Combe') e.g. Castle Combe or Ilfracombe – it comes from 'Cymb' which means valley.

The Romans
Aye, they left their mark too. The Latin word 'Castrum' became 'Chester' and 'Caster', giving us places such as Chester itself and Bicester, Chichester, Gloucester, Manchester and Winchester – it indicates there used to be a military site there.

The Anglo-Saxons

The (Germanic) Angles and Saxons got together once the Romans left our isles, around the 5th century. And lasted until about 1066, when the Normans invaded. It is these Angles who give us the very name, England and the region of East Anglia. The Saxons gave us the regions (now counties), Middlesex, Wessex and Sussex (Middle, West and South Saxons).

Getting back to town names, though…they gave us **'Ham'** e,g, Birmingham, Durham and Nottingham – it stems from the Old English 'ham', meaning home/homestead/farm/settlement.

'Ton' is another popular one from their era e.g. Bolton, Luton, Northampton and Southampton – 'tun' meaning farm/enclosure/village.

'Worth' was a Saxon enclosure e.g. Kenilworth, Knebworth and Tamworth – If we take Kenilworth, it was an enclosure belonging to a Saxon woman named Cynehild.

Towns with **'mouth'** indicate the mouth of a river e.g. Exmouth or Plymouth. Or 'burna' which became **'burn'** and **'bourne'** meant a brook e.g. Blackburn, Eastbourne and Glyndebourne.

Religious settlements for clergy received a **'minster'** e.g. Axminster, Kidderminster and Westminster. Or **'stow'** as in Chepstow, Felixstowe or Padstow.

Norse

The Vikings (Norsemen) invaded, and their 8th-11th century influence can be found in places with a **'by'** e.g. Corby or Whitby – the 'by' being Norse for village.

So, you can combine a direction or natural feature, perhaps with roots to an old name and create your own place name.

- Bourne
- By
- Cester
- Combe
- Ham
- Minster
- Mouth
- Pen
- Ton
- Worth

Alternatively, find a random actual place name without a duke, earl etc. and give them one (a noble, that is).

It's up to you. How creative do you feel?

15th CENTURY DETAILS

INTRODUCTION TO THE 15th CENTURY

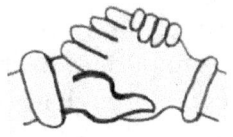

Before we begin on our deep-dive into 15th century England, I wanted to take a breath and gather our thoughts.

Hopefully, by going through the first section of this book, you've reached a better understanding of your 'when'. Maybe you've even narrowed your time setting down to a year. This is important. You need to know what was going on around them.

I appreciate all of that got a bit 'information heavy' — it is what it is. Although this next section looks more closely into 15th century life, I hope you find the mood a bit lighter.

So, next in my approach to research, we come across **'what'**. I cover this in more detail in, *How To Write A Historical Novel And Love It*, but you are probably writing either a historical fiction or a historical romance novel.

Basically, romance demands a HEA (happily ever after) or at least a HFN (happy for now), and everything revolves around the romantic relationship/love. Whereas historical fiction focuses on events.

Incidentally, if you're writing a fantasy novel, you'll need to decide if it's a high/low one. Or, maybe it's a historical, paranormal or dark fantasy. Is it a sword & sorcery? Same rule applies; if the love story is the pivotal feature, it's probably a romantic fantasy.

The **'why'** questions are also covered in *How To Write A Historical Novel And Love It*. Your own reasons for writing are deeply personal and entirely up to you. There are no right or wrong answers. But it is important to know your motives as these will help sustain you through the tougher times of writing.

What we are left with then is the 'where' and 'who'. We've already looked at town vs country and the spread of agricultural workers vs merchants. And we'll look into their housing situation in a moment.

In this section, we'll be looking into **'who'** your characters are:

- their names
- the houses they lived in
- what they ate and when
- farming practices
- the medical care available for whatever diseases they may contract
- their general hygiene
- how women coped
- a closer look at religion
- how they told the time
- what spending power their money had
- which servants did what
- writing and education
- how law was implemented
- the clothes they wore
- knights and weaponry
- how people travelled
- what they did for amusement
- some fun insults and compliments

All of these things go into creating who your characters are and how they live and interact with one another.

Deep breath. Ready? Alright, let's go...

NAMES

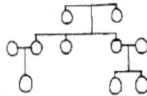

I'm going to start with popular names, as it's one of the most common gripes readers seem to have with historical books. It completely throws readers out of the story when modern names creep in.

Fun Fact: If you look up the meaning/etymology of my main character's names, they give you a heavy hint as to their character/role in the story. Yes, I'm that geek.

So, let me list some of the most popular names in 15th century England. The top 100 in each boys and girls, in alphabetical order. Flip the page; I've put them into a table which hopefully makes it clearer.

Boys Names

Abel	Abraham	Adam	Adrian	Alexander
Allan	Ambrose	Ames	Andrew	Anthony
Arthur	Austin / Augustine	Barnaby / Barnabas	Bartholomew	Benjamin
Bernard	Brian	Charles	Christopher	Clement
Cuthbert	Daniel	David	Edmund	Edward
Elias / Ellis	Emanuel	Erasmus	Evan	Ferdinando
Francis	Fulke	Gabriel	Geoffrey	George
Gerard / Garret	Gilbert	Giles	Gregory	Griffith / Griffin
Henry	Herbert	Hugh	Humphrey	Isaac
James	Jarvis / Gervase	Jasper / Gaspar	Jeffrey / Geoffrey	Jeremy
Jerome	John	Jonah / Jonas	Joseph	Joshua
Josiah / Josias	Lancelot	Laurence	Lawrence	Leonard
Lewis	Lionel	Luke	Mark	Marmaduke
Martin	Mathias / Matthias / Matthew	Michael	Miles	Morgan
Morris / Maurice	Nathaniel	Nicholas	Oliver	Owen
Paul	Peter / Peirs / Pers	Philip	Ralph	Randall / Randolph
Reginald / Reynold	Richard	Robert	Roderic	Roger
Roland / Rowland	Sampson / Samson	Samuel	Simon	Stephen
Theophilus	Thomas	Timothy	Toby / Tobias	Tristram
Valentine	Vincent	Walter	William	Zachary

Girls Names

Adelina	Agnes	Alice	Alma	Althea
Alyson	Amelina	Amy	Anne	Artemisia
Athelina	Audrey	Augusta	Avis	Barbara
Beatrice	Bertha	Blanche	Bridget	Cassandra
Catelin	Catherine / Katherine	Cecily	Celestria	Charity
Christina	Clare	Clarice	Clemence	Constance
Dameta	Delia	Dorothy	Edith	Elaine
Eleanor / Elinor	Elizabeth	Ellen	Emma	Eva
Evaine	Felicia	Floria / Flora / Florence	Fortune	Frances
Frideswide	Genevieve	Gillian	Gisela / Giselle	Grace
Guinevere	Gwendolen	Helen	Ida	Ingerid
Isabel / Isobel	Isemay	Isolda	Ivette	Jane
Janet	Joan	Johanna	Joyce	Judith
Juliana	Justina	Lena	Leticia / Letia	Lia
Lillian	Lucy / Lucia	Mabel	Magdalen	Margaret / Margery
Marion	Martha	Mary	Mathilde	Maud
Milicent	Miriel / Muriel	Nicola	Olivia	Paulina
Phillippa	Rachel	Regina	Roana	Rose / Rosa / Rosamund
Sabina	Sarah	Susanna	Sybil	Thomasin
Thora	Ursula	Venetia	Viviane	Ysmeine

Of course, these don't indicate which social class or region. But they at least won't be jarring. Biblical names were still popular, so when in doubt, go with them.

Surnames

These are a whole other matter. Did you know that surnames weren't really a thing in England until 1066? At least, so rumour has it.

They can be grouped into four categories; occupation, patronymic (from their father), topographic (of the land) or nicknames.

They were a way of differentiating one 'John' from another when the population grew. But I don't think people generally used them in everyday speech. So, I wouldn't worry too much.

However, I don't want to leave you hanging, so I'll give a few ideas:

Abbott	Armstrong	Baker	Bannister	Barker
Beamish	Bedford	Blake	Bourke	Bourne
Burrows	Chapman	Fiddler	Fleming	Fox
Frobisher	Goldsmith	Goodchild	Hampshire	Harper
Hill	Hobson	Hornblower	Leech	Littlejohn
Mason	Milner	Moore	Oakham	Piper
Plummer	Pope	Smith	Thatcher	White
Wilkinson	Willamson	Wold	Wood	Wright

Nobles do loathe being ordinary. They had slightly different surnames. If they emigrated from France, one would see them add 'de' (of) and their placename e.g. de Burgh.

The rich folk usually used their titles anyway.

Hopefully, this at least points you in the right direction.

Writing Prompt - Name

A character walks into the room and introduces themselves.

- What is the name of your main character?
- What do they call their main friend?
- Name your antagonist. Is it something harsh and evil sounding?
- Do their names have a hidden meaning? (It's OK if you just like the name)

You may also like to give them some features at this point:

- What colour hair and eyes do they have?
- Are they short or tall (in comparison to their contemporaries)?

Maybe find some images somewhere like Pinterest and save them in a file to give yourself a good idea of what they look like. Clothing will be covered later in this section; don't panic.

WHO'S IN CHARGE?

Let us briefly refresh the list of monarchs, but keep it within the 15th century:

PLANTAGENETS

House of Lancaster
- Henry IV / Henry of Bolingbroke: 1399 – 1413 (usurper)
- Henry V / Henry of Monmouth: 1413 – 1422

The Wars of the Roses (1455 – 1485) then sees a lot of back and forth between the Plantagenet houses of Lancaster and York:
- Henry VI (Lancaster): 1422-1461
- Edward IV (York): 1461-1470
- Henry VI (again): 1470-1471 (imprisoned & died)
- Edward IV (again): 1471-1483 (died)
- Edward V: Apr-Jun 1483
  (not crowned & mysteriously disappeared along with his brother, aka The Princes in the Tower)
- Richard III (York): 1483-1485

Then, at the tail end of the 15th century, enter in:
House of Tudor (1485 – 1603)
- Henry VII (Tudor): 1485-1509

That's the 7th, and not his son who had 6 wives.

You can see why I did this, right? There are a lot of changes. I mean, compare this to the late Queen Elizabeth II who ruled for over 70 years. Most of us have only known one monarch in the UK until very recently.

So, nine changes within a 100-year period seems to reflect the turmoil of the times. And it's important to know who's on the throne, even if they're not the focus of your story.

But don't forget the Pope is technically above all. I'll expand on religion a bit later.

Would you like quick **highlights of each of these kings**? Let's go for it.

Henry IV / Henry of Bolingbroke: 1399 – 1413
- Usurped the throne
- First English king to speak English as his primary language
- Faced many uprisings/rebellions throughout his reign
- Fought at the Battle of Shrewsbury in 1403
- Was ill from 1405, and his son played more of a role in government

His reign is viewed as one of turmoil, and that he was a competent yet troubled monarch.

Henry V / Henry of Monmouth: 1413 – 1422
- Son of Henry IV
- Gained victories in France e.g. Battle of Agincourt
- 1420 Treaty of Troyes declared him heir to the French throne
- Married Charles VI's (of France) daughter, Catherine of Valois
- 1422 – died of dysentery in France

Viewed as a pious man and a brilliant military leader. He was ruthless but strengthened English identity, although he did rather neglect domestic affairs.

Henry VI (Lancaster): 1422-1461 and 1470-1471

- Became king at 8 months old, therefore had to rely on people around him:
  His uncles: Humphrey, Duke of Gloucester, became Regent of England
  and John, Duke of Bedford, Regent of France
- Richard Beauchamp, Earl of Warwick, was his tutor
- His mother remarried, to Welshman, Owen Tudor - their son, Edmund, Earl of Richmond, became the father of the first Tudor King, Henry VI – she died in 1437
- Crowned King of England in 1429 (age 7).
- 1431 - also crowned King of France (only English monarch to hold both crowns)
- 1440 – Founded Eton College then King's College, Cambridge in 1442
- 1445 – diplomatically married Margaret of Anjou (niece to Charles VII of France)
- Lost Normandy, France in 1450, thanks partly to Joan of Arc
- 1453 – he became ill, and Richard, Duke of York, was made Protector in 1454 (recovered 1455)
- 1461 – deposed
- 1470 – restored to the throne but deposed again 1471 when he was imprisoned in the Tower of London where he suddenly died (probably murdered)

Generally viewed as a weak, passive, mentally unstable king. Lack of military prowess. But was pious and favoured diplomacy and education. Got blamed for the Wars of the Roses.

Edward IV (York): 1461-1470 and 1471-1483

- Claimed the throne after the Battle of Towton in 1461 (Henry VI fled to Scotland with his wife)
- 1464 – married Elizabeth Woodville (her 2nd marriage) for love and against advice (they had 10 children together, including Edward V)
- 1470 - the Earl of Warwick, aka 'the Kingmaker', turned on him and switched to the other side along with Edward's own brother! Deposed fled to the Low Countries.
- But then Edward won the battles of Barnet (where the Earl of Warwick got killed; oops!) and the Battle of Tewkesbury, and regained the throne in 1471, imprisoning King Henry VI (see previous king).
- 1475 - Made peace with France
- Personally, 'sat on the bench' to enforce justice, and managed state finances (reduced debt)
- Encouraged commercial treaties, and restored his family's fortunes in the process via the wool trade (did not rely on parliamentary subsidies)
- Patronised the development of the printing press, and collected books
- 1483 – died possibly from poisoning, or maybe malaria, syphilis or pneumonia

Viewed as a strong military leader and a charmer with financial acumen but led a lavish lifestyle and misjudged some political situations.

Edward V: Apr-Jun 1483 (not crowned & mysteriously disappeared along with his brother, aka The Princes in the Tower)

Richard III (York): 1483-1485
This one's going to get complex!
- Brother to Edward IV
- Upon his brother's death, Richard, Duke of Gloucester became Lord Protector for his nephew (Edward V) but then declared him & his siblings illegitimate
- The two princes then became legend: they were escorted to The Tower of London "for their protection" – but nobody quite knows what happened to them
- 1483 - Richard then became king, with support from parliament
- His laws were written entirely in English (for the 1st time ever), making them fairer and less liable to corruption
- Reformed the jury system
- Introduced 'bail' which we still use today, and he often ruled in favour of 'the common man'
- Encouraged trade and the printing industry
- His wife, Anne Neville, the younger daughter of the 'King Maker' Earl of Warwick (married 1472), died March 1485 – their son died the year before
- There were rumours he wanted to marry his (illegitimate) niece, Elizabeth of York, but it appears he wanted her to marry a minor Portuguese royal
- The last English monarch to die on the battlefield (at the Battle of Bosworth in August 1485, age 32)

There are definitely two camps: those who believe he killed the Princes in the Tower and usurped the throne, and those who do not. We will never know the actual truth. I advise you to merely pick a side that you believe most – both have solid arguments.

We now know he was not deformed, as Tudor propaganda would have us believe, so what other lies did they spin? They definitely muddied the waters.

But look, he at least did some good in his short reign.

Obviously, **Henry VII begins the Tudor dynasty** (reign: 1485-1509), so falls outside the scope of the medieval era this book is focused on.

However… he fathered Henry VIII, and was rather shrewd if not terribly popular. Definitely a better king than his son was, though.

Writing Prompt – King

The church bells ring out for the coronation of…?

- So, who's on the throne in your book?
- Are they well liked?
- What were their greatest achievements?
- What villainy have the committed?
- Is your main character a supporter or opposer of their monarch? (this choice may be clearer later on)

HOUSING

One of the next important questions should be where your character/s live.

Obviously, the quality of one's abode depended very much on your social class. But even the homes of the peasants may not have been as dreadful as we first thought.

Of course, plumbing was yet to be invented. And central heating was eons away. But straw rooves were quite effective, and fires were in every household. Also, walls were good and thick.

In my research for *Love in the Roses*, I was looking at the sort of dwelling in which one would find a knight who lived the countryside. This would have been a manor house.

So, let's take a closer look into the rooms you'd expect to find in those.

Rooms of a 15th Century Manor House

Most importantly, there was the **Great Hall**. At the time, this would have just been called the hall, incidentally. This was where the lord and lady of the house would entertain their guests. As such, it would be the most highly decorated room.

The floor would have reeds covering it, with herbs also strewn to help with the smell. After all, these reeds were not changed very often, and food would probably get spilled (*bleurgh!*).

Tapestries would hang on the walls — for decoration but also warmth and to hide any visual signs of damp. Family banners may also be hung about, displaying the family's coat of arms if they had one i.e. they were a knight.

A hearth would provide the warmth of a large fire, and large windows would let in daylight. A dais could stand proud for the most distinguished guests who would sit at the top table with chairs. Trestle tables and benches were laid out for others, filtering down in order of rank.

A minstrels' gallery may stand above the Great Hall, along the rear wall. As it suggests, this would be a place for the minstrels to play, entertaining the guests.

This would also be the room where household servants would sleep. The presence of the fireplace meant it was relatively warm. They would probably make their bed by stuffing sacks with hay and laying it on the floor. Some may also have slept in the kitchen.

The **screens passage** would lead guests in/out of the Great Hall. This hid the comings and goings as it led to the chapel, kitchen, buttery and pantry.

Morning Mass would be heard daily by the household in the **chapel**. Stained glass windows would be a feature. An oratory, a smaller private chapel may run off from the chapel, for private family prayers.

The **kitchen** may be a separate building, connected by a passage or it could be part of the manor building (in later houses). Most of the food preparation and cooking would be done in here.

Out the other side of the kitchen, was the kitchen garden, so the cooks had easy access to the vegetables and herbs.

Here, you'll also find a **scullery** in its own building. Clothes and dishes were washed here, and ironing was done. It is also where water was heated for bathing and cooking.

The **pantry**, near the kitchen, was used to store perishable foods and to prepare bread.

The **buttery**, in the same area as the kitchen and pantry, was where ale and candles were stored.

Often, a staircase led down to the **bottlery**/wine cellar (the wine store). This is where we get the word butler, by the way; from the Anglo-French *buteillier*, cup-bearer / officer in charge of wine,

A **granary** would house grain, again, separately.

Also outside, you would find **stables**, a **fishpond** (fish were kept for the table; not ornamental) and maybe even a **dovecote**. There should also be a **well** so one could collect fresh drinking water.

The Lord's **bath** was a stone chamber nearby. Baths were large wooden barrels, which servants would fill with heated water and herbs. A lead pipe may have carried wastewater away. Complete with a dressing area and ledges for accessories, presumably not a rubber ducky though (*giggle*).

Back through the house and the Great Hall, we find a **laver**. A stone basin built into the wall. A tank was filled above from buckets, and a tap allowed guests to wash their hands before and after meals. A pipe carried the water away.

Shall we climb the stairs? Yes, in the later medieval period, a **bedchamber** or **solar** would be reached on the second storey. Tapestries would adorn the walls.

An ornately carved **bed** would be in situ, with linen hangings which could be drawn at night to keep the warmth in. A feather mattress would sit atop rope or leather strapping, as well as a coverlet and blankets. Pillows and bolster cushions would be piled high, as sleeping in a more upright position was considered good practice.

There would probably be a canopy (curtain), but not in the form of a four-poster bed. It was more likely to be suspended from poles which hung from the ceiling. Or, possibly a box bed, which was enclosed by wooden panels — almost a room within a room vibe.

To warm the bed, a stone or brick could be placed in the fireplace, wrapped in fabric and placed in the bed.

A trundle bed would be stowed under the main one and could be pulled out for chamber servants.

Fun fact: beds were incredibly expensive, treasured items which would be passed on through wills. This is more in reference to the ornately carved, wooden ones in manor houses. One would proudly display these, hence the business dealings happening in this room.

And, btw, children would share this bed with their parents. Or they may have taken the place of the servant on the truckle/trundle bed. There weren't many rooms and one wished to keep warm. Possibly another reason children were sent away from around age 7?

Final note on beds — these were made to be portable. If the lord of the manor had to travel to one of his other properties, his staff would pack up his bed, and even maybe the windows to set up wherever he resided.

The fire in the bedchamber would keep the room warm, yet posed a fire hazard, given the wooden floors (with more reeds strewn on).

The large windows in this room gave it the alternative name of **solar**; they allowed light in. Much business would be conducted in this room, so you may also reasonably find a desk.

In larger homes, an area of the solar may be sectioned off as the **bower**. This was the lady's private chamber. Embroidery or entertaining may happen in here. This later became the withdrawing room.

Also, leading off of the solar was the **wardrobe**. This was the area for the lord and lady to dress. The chamberlain would store the fine clothes, expensive spices, money, plate and jewellery in here, and dressmaking was conducted.

The **garderobe/privy** was located within or adjacent to the wardrobe. Yes, this was the toilet. A glorified hole, with probably a plank of wood atop it (also with a hole in). Some jutted out of the house wall on a platform. But they all had to lead somewhere; chutes took the...err..waste down to a cesspit or moat. Both of these would need to be cleared out every so often – what a lovely job that must've been!?

NB Moated houses were decreasing in popularity, partly because of the associated stench and it attracted nasties like bugs and rats. So, not many manor houses were moated in the 15th century.

Straw or rags were used for...**wiping**. Sometimes, a damp sponge on a stick. A window was happily situated to help alleviate the odour. Bars were in situ to stop intruders entering via the chutes.

Chamber pots were also used, by the way.

Oh dear, am I really talking about toilets? How unseemly!

NB None of these rooms were large. Even the Great Hall was probably smaller than you're imagining. Stone houses were often cold and damp, so keeping heat in was a prime consideration.

It's actually very difficult to find an authentic house from the era as 99% have been added to over the years as they were just too small.

But there you have it: a guided tour of a 15th century manor house.

Was there anything you found surprising in here?

Castles

Castles had similar rooms to manor houses, but in a different layout and were fortified.

There would also have been a **keep** (the central part). The tallest tower, which at the time was probably called a **don-jon** (not dungeon) — its French origin meant 'stronghold'.

It would have had a moat.

Entrance would have been via the **barbican**; a narrow passageway jutting out from the gatehouse. This was an important part of the castle's defence, and may also have arrow-slits and/or pots of boiling oil etc. to fend off attackers.

Additionally, there were other watch towers, battlements, rampart, and some sort of prison room (not really a dungeon).

The **inner courtyard** would have been used for knights' training and events. And an **outer courtyard** would have housed animals.

Peasant Housing

Well, this won't take as long to look around.

During the 14th century, half-timbered houses started to emerge. However, for those living in poverty, not much timber would have been used, and most likely were made mostly of cob, especially in the south-west of England which has more sandy soil.

Cob is basically constructed with a stone base with a lot of mud shovelled on top which was then trodden down. This formed the walls. One could then add a layer of plaster to help keep the cold and damp out.

Peasant housing was basic, but not as pokey as you may think. Walking in, you may find yourself in the **inner room** where the fire was — there was probably no oven, though. There may be a sectioned off area at one end for **storage**, and another at the other end for **sleeping**.

Beds in peasant houses by the 15th century *could* be raised off the floor by means of a wooden frame. Whether on a frame or not, mattresses would be stuffed with straw, hay, wool or rags. They may have a single blanket. This was more commonly referred to as a **cot** than a bed.

Maybe more so in villages, there were **hall houses** which had an upstairs. The buttery and pantry would have been downstairs, again with the fire being central. And the solar or bed chamber would have been on the upper level.

Shops in villages would have had living quarters above them.

The better paid craftsmen would have lived in the nicer houses in the village. Including woodcutters - apparently, they didn't live in little cabins in the woods. (*Boo!*)

Monasteries

You're probably not going to need too much detail on monasteries. Not many authors are as crazy as me and decide to base their book in one. However, your character may stay in the guest house of one overnight.

Whilst researching *Love Habit*, I gathered a lot of information. Most monasteries followed the same basic floorplan. I drew this cute map:

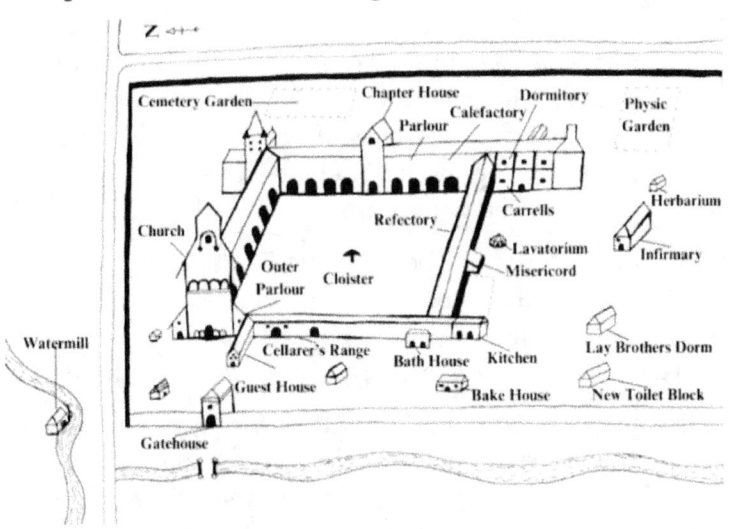

Fig 1: Layout of a monastery drawn by TL Clark

I've labelled the main areas one would require.

The **cloister** formed the central part of the monastery. Other rooms were then located along this perimeter: the chapter house, parlour, calefactory (warming room), refectory, kitchen, cellarer's range and the church.

NB The calefactory was one of the only rooms to hold a hearth fire. These places were freezing cold in winter!

The **infirmary** was its own separate building and also had a fireplace as the sick needed to be kept warm and concoctions had to be heated. There may be a separate section in here for the frail elderly monks who were no longer able to move about easily and were excused from most work and services.

Monasteries were like mini cities and contained most of the everyday needs of the inhabitants. A **bakehouse** and **brewery** ensured a steady supply of bread and ale; staples of their diet. And a stew pond would have housed fish, but more would have been bought in.

Stables would also have been situated outside of the precinct but may have contained more donkeys than horses. Although, the families offering teenaged sons into the monastery were rich, so it's likely horses would be there too.

There was a **dormitory** to the south of the precinct. This was supposed to be a communal sleeping room for the monks who each had a small bed there. However, as we're looking at the 15th century, the monks had often managed to get a nice bed fitted in their working area. This afforded them more privacy and convenience. After all, who wants to sleep in a room with a whole load of snoring, farting men?

Lighting

Whichever type of building you were in, one required some form of lighting.

Candles

Let's start with the humble candle. (*snickers, knowing how else they were used in *Love Habit**).

Most candles were made from animal fat or tallow (rendered suet) from cows or sheep. They stank! But it was cheaper than beeswax, so one put up with the smoky flame.

The nobility could afford the clean, pleasant beeswax candles. And churches used them for liturgical purposes. Monasteries often had beehives; great for producing beeswax as well as honey. But even so, England imported a lot of beeswax from Eastern Europe in the Middle Ages.

I briefly mention coil candles in the 'time' section later. They were effectively a length of cotton string dipped in beeswax and coiled round.

Rushlights

As it sounds, lights made of rushes – these reeds grew abundantly in medieval England. Peasants could harvest then dry them, strip the outer coating to use the central pith as a wick. This wick was dipped in rendered animal fat and left to dry. Once ready, they could be mounted in metal pincer-type holders called nips. Some nips also had a candle holder mount so either type could be used.

This was as cheap as you could get, made of materials serfs could easily lay their hands on.

A 15 inch long rushlight could burn for half an hour, or one which was two and a half feet long could burn for an hour. And gave a good light.

Fun fact: UK folk were still using rushlights into the 19th century.

Lamps

There were several types of lamps.

Hanging Lamps – included chandeliers and lanterns.

Chandeliers could be small and simple, or large and ornate. Usually found in Great Halls or churches.

Lanterns tended to be smaller. They could be hung up on chains, or handheld and carried around; good for journeys.

Table Lamps

Upon one's table, one could have a candlestick (or two) or an oil lamp.

I've already detailed candles themselves.

So, let's look at **oil lamps**. They could be made from clay or wood, but were again, an expensive option. But they did burn for a good length of time (longer than candles). And a pretty red oil lamp could give a romantic glow in one's bedchamber (*swit swoo*).

Sadly, supply of olive oil was limited and costly. So, a lot of English folk burned belly or kidney fat from pigs or cows instead. Smelly and sooty!

Wall Lamps

Wall sconces held decorative lamps, and were usually used to highlight décor, as the light was soft and warm.

Dragons and other mythical beasts may have been used to decorate these lamps, especially in castles. Whilst religious figures were depicted in others.

They were usually made of iron in homes. But some churches used bronze.

NB They **did not** have torches on the walls! Movies again have lied.

Torches

Let's clear this up. Torches were a length of wood with some coarse fabric e.g. jute wrapped around one end. The fabric would have been dipped in fat, oil, beeswax or pitch.

Hand-held torches, like one sees in movies, would only have burned for 10-30 minutes. That's it! Not great for roaming long distances with. I know it's a fun image. So, look, I won't judge you if your character brandishes one, but do please appreciate it's unrealistic.

If one had a man-sized torch, it would have needed a stand to hold it but could burn for up to two hours. These were not generally used indoors.

Heating

Braziers

I just wanted to quickly mention braziers. These were portable metal containers, usually holding hot coals. Mainly used for heating rooms which had no hearth/fireplace. But some included a grill for cooking on.

They were also used in religious or ceremonial ways too.

Braziers could be tall or squat, some had tripod stands whilst others just had little feet. Some were ornate whilst others were more like cages built from iron strips.

Very versatile and handy things.

Other than these, fires in hearths or **fireplaces** were used to keep rooms warm.

Writing Prompt – Housing

Your character goes home at the end of a long day. What do they see?

- Does your MC live in the countryside or town?
- What type of house do they live in?
- How many rooms are there?
- Where does your MC sleep, and is it comfy?
- And how brightly is it lit?
- How warm are they?

FOOD OF 15th CENTURY ENGLAND

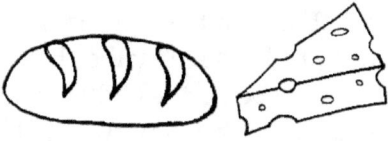

Mmmm…One of my favourite topics, and actually one which will help set the scene for your characters. Food plays a crucial role in our lives that we often don't appreciate these days.

What will your characters eat?

Food was definitely only available on a seasonal basis. Yep, we had to rely on what we could get. Wellaway, the days before supermarkets and globalisation! To be fair, even in my own childhood, there was a more limited, seasonal choice, but then I am middle-aged.

Rule number 1: **there were**

NO POTATOES, TOMATOES, TEA OR COFFEE!

I know, it pained me too. Just how did they survive? I don't wake up without coffee. And I eat some form of potato product every day (*back of hand flies to forehead*).

Time and time again, I've discovered recipes citing they've come from *The Forme of Cury*. That's because it's one of the earliest if not *the* first known English cooking recipe book. It was compiled around 1390-1420 by the chief Master Cooks of King Richard II. *Cury* being the Old French for cookery, not the spicy cuisine of our modern world. It's a very useful reference for those wanting insight into rich people's food.

With apologies to vegetarian, vegan and generally sensitive readers, but meat (flesh) formed a large part of the rich person's diet. The poor tended to only eat bits of meat when they could, so had a more 'bread and veg' menu.

NB Wednesdays, Fridays and Saturdays were meat-free for everyone.

For the rich, this meant eating fish. For the poor, well, it was life as normal, really.

Taking into account all the Lent and fast days, one could only consume meat around 50% of the year.

Funnily enough, the flesh days were more popular – you'd expect more guests to dinner. Unless they were friars, who made a point of only visiting on fish days due to their vows to never eat flesh. Sundays were generally the busiest dinner days, when guests could include clergy, social peers, estate workers and officials – women were more likely to appear on Sundays too. Followed by Thursdays in popularity. Saturdays were least popular.

Outside of those days, the nobles could eat:

- Every month – beef and pork
- Most months – venison
- Dec-Aug – veal
- Dec- Jul – suckling pig (but only on fancy occasions)
- Summer – lamb and mutton (with none at all mid Feb to the end of May).
- Pigeon was also summer only
- Proper high status folk also ate swan and heron

Chicken (hen or capon), pheasant, partridge, duck and goose were commonly eaten by the nobility. Sometimes, they may include blackbird, bustard, crane, heron or plover.

Rabbits are slightly controversial as there is contradictory evidence when they were re-/introduced (it was probably the Romans), and they struggled to breed at first (ironic, eh?). But we do know **coney** was on the menu – these were bunnies bred for the table. And some people say, the peasants were allowed to hunt hares and rabbits (but no other animals).

Cute bunnies were highly prized for their flesh *and* fur, and so they were farmed. Some noble houses had warrens, but oh look, monasteries were apparently good rabbit farmers — must have been lucrative!

And don't forget **venison** – sorry, Bambi! Deer parks were kept for the lords to go hunting – sport and food purposes.

Bacon deserves a special mention. We were eating it as far back as the Saxon era. It was a specific cut of pork loin or belly from certain breeds which was salted/cured. What we now call back bacon is basically what it was even then. And was even sometimes eaten by peasants – huzzah!

Swine (pigs) were able to wander around woodlands freely, foraging for themselves, so they were a lot cheaper to raise. But the wealthy did also eat pork.

Game Seasons

I couldn't source any accurate game season records from the era, so when writing, I tend to use this more modern version, as things don't seem to have changed too much in terms of when one can hunt.

Birds
- **Red Grouse**   12 August - 10 December
- **Partridge**   1 September - 1 February
- **Pheasant**   1 October - 1 February
- **Pigeon**   No closed season

Wild Fowl
- **Ducks**   1 September - 31 January
- **Snipe**   12 August - 31 January
- **Woodcock**   1 October - 31 January

Furred
- **Hare**   1 January - 31 December
  ~ but can only be *sold* between 1 August and 28 February
- **Rabbit**   No closed season
- **Squirrel**   No closed season

Venison (England & Wales)
- **Muntjac Deer** No closed season
- **Roe Deer**   Bucks: 1 Apr - 31 Oct
                    Does: 1 Nov - 31 March
- **Fallow Deer** Bucks: 1 Aug - 30 April
                    Does: 1 Nov - 31 March
- **Red Deer**   Stags: 1 Aug - 30 Apr
                    Hinds: 1 Nov - 31 March

Boar
No closed season

NB The word 'meat' just meant food at this time. 'Flesh' was used to describe land animal dishes.

Fish

- **Herrings** (bought in bulk) – smoked red herrings were cheaper than pickled white ones.
- **Barrels of salmon or sturgeon** could be bought if herrings were in short supply.
- **Salt fish** and stockfish were regularly served.
- **Oysters** were plentiful but went up by ½ d at Christmas due to increased demand!
  And not eaten between May and the end of Aug ("never eat an oyster unless there's an 'r' in the month") because that's when they become poisonous.
- **Eels** may have been supplied from stew ponds on estates.

- **Folk living on the coast**: brill, butts (a flat fish; stop sniggering), cod, crabs, crayfish, flathe, garfish, haddock, mackerel, merling (whiting), mussels, oysters, plaice, sea-pike, shrimps, skate, sole, sparling, turbot, and/or welks

- **Folk living inland near freshwater**: bream, eels, salmon, tench and trout

What else could be fish?

Well, with so many fish days, especially during Lent, one would get ever so weary of the above listed fish. It's understandable that they flexed the definition. So, seabirds who had ^obviously^ been created at sea, were included as fish e.g. puffins and barnacle geese.

Other animals got included — if it lived in water it was clearly a fish; beaver tails, dolphins and porpoises. Oh, my!

Cheese

Even cheese seems to have controversy around it. However, it is possible these cheeses were available, either made locally or imported from Europe / 'The Continent' by rich folk.

Word of caution – a lot of cheese didn't store or travel well, so would have been more of a local treat.

- **Beaufort** (aging 6-14months) - French, firm elastic texture
- **Brie** (3-6 weeks) – French, soft
- **Cheddar** (2 months to 2 years age) – Somerset, England, hard. First recorded use is in 1500 but probably around before that. Confusingly, it wasn't actually called Cheddar until 1655.
- **Emmenthal** (6-14months) – Swiss, semi-hard
- **Farmer's Cheese** - a soft, pressed cottage cheese; unripened curd. Uncertain origin, made in Middle East and Europe from almost any milk. A common cheese at this time.
- **Feta** – Crete, Greek, soft, crumbly goat's or sheep's milk, curd cheese aged in brine. Originally called "*prosphatos*"; the name "feta" started in 17th century. But mentioned in some form in Homer's *Odyssey* in 8th century BC.
- **Grana** – Italian, hard, crumbly (similar to parmesan). First recorded in 1200.
- **Gorgonzola** – Italian, blue cheese, first recorded in 879.
- **Gruyére** (6 months age) – Swiss / Alpine, medium-hard, yellow.
- **Maroilles, Mozzarella** (non-aged) – Italian, semi-soft made from buffalo milk. Possibly first made in the 8th (or 12th) century by monks in the Campania

region near Naples. But 1st century Romans made something similar using sheep's milk.
- **Parmesan / Parmigiano-Reggiano** (12-24 months) – Italian, hard, granular. First recorded in 1200 made by monks who used local salt as a preservative. Traded more widely from around 14th century.
- **Reblochon** – French (Alpine region), soft, washed-rind, creamy. First recorded use in the 14th century but localised as it was a sneaky way to avoid milk taxation (from a second milking).
- **Rowen/Ruayn(e) (many various spellings)** – Thought to be Anglo-Norman. It is later mentioned in *The Forme of Cury* (so, at the very least, 14th century). Autumn cheese, made after the cattle had fed on the second growth (the "rowen"). This was a semi-soft cheese, but not as soft as a ripe modern Brie.
- **Ricotta** – Italian, whey cheese. Seems to have Ancient Roman influence origins.
- **Pecorino Romano** (5-12 months) – Italian, hard, salty made from sheep's milk. With origins around 300BC. One of the oldest cheeses in the world!
- **Roquefort** (3-4 months) – French, blue cheese made from Lacaune ewe's milk, aged in the caves of Roquefort-sur-Soulzon. Semi-soft, crumbly, tangy. Recorded in 79AD – one of the oldest known cheeses.
- **(Sussex) Slipcote** –Sussex, England. Soft, ewe cheese, fluffy with a citrus flavour. "Since the Middle Ages" is the claim of origin.
- **Spermyse** aka Green Cheese – English, soft or cream cheese flavoured with herbs, made and eaten in the summer. Sorry, I have no date, just that it was "medieval".

The reason I mention all of the above diverse cheeses is because the knowledge was there. And monks seem to have been great cheesemakers. So, when they first came to England from France in the 6th century, they may have brought some of that know-how with them and even expanded upon it throughout the ages. Monks did sometimes travel between monasteries; it was a great information network.

There was also a great tradition of cheesemaking in England, more from ewe's milk, on local estate farms. The lords then traded some of that produce.

Fun fact: Cheese could be viewed as medicinal. Bald's *Leechbook* suggests eating new cheese and wheat bread for those suffering from a penetrating intestinal worm, or cheese and honey for dysentery. And even a "wit-sick person" (someone who's gone a bit loopy?), was to eat blessed bread and cheese with garlic and cropleek. Generally, it was seen as a useful digestive at the end of each meal — probably why the cheese course still exists today.

Vegetables

I've often seen it said that nobles thought vegetables were merely what their food should eat, and thus snubbed them. I'm not sure how true that statement is, but they definitely had a meat rich diet (hence all the gout).

The peasants didn't get the choice. Most meat was too expensive. They may occasionally manage to get a bit of pork or mutton. But they mainly grew vegetables in their own gardens (tofts). Typical examples of vegetables:

- Cabbages
- Chard
- Garlic
- Leeks
- Onions
- Parsnips
- Peas
- Spinach
- Turnips

One of the advantages of most of these was their long storage time.

Remember NO POTATOES (*whimper*)!

Vetches have been grown in Kent since around 1238, but it seems other regions didn't get them until the 14th century. Either way, 15th century writers are safe. There are around 140 varieties of this leguminous crop belonging to the pea family. I mention them as they were useful fodder (food for livestock). And helped retain the quality of the soil. Just in case you needed to know.

Fruit

Fruit could be enjoyed by all. Apples, pears and plums were perhaps most commonly found. Delicious in pies, used as a sweetener, or as jam.

The English fruit harvesting times were generally (weather dependent):

- **June** – gooseberries, redcurrants, rhubarb, strawberries.
- **July** – blackcurrants, cherries, gooseberries, loganberries, raspberries, redcurrants, rhubarb, strawberries, tayberries, white currants.
- **August** – early-season apples, blackberries, blackcurrants, cherries, plums, raspberries, strawberries, tayberries.
- **September** – mid-season apples, blackberries, elderberries, plums, raspberries, strawberries.
- **October** – mid-season apples, elderberries, pears, plums, raspberries, strawberries.
- **November** – late-season apples.

Eggs and Poultry

Many rural houses had **a cockerel and around five hens**. These were mainly used for their eggs as a useful supplement to their diet. This was actually jolly sensible, as eggs are high in protein and vitamins – very nutritious!

Many richer dishes also included hard boiled eggs. So, it seems everyone ate them.

The nobles also ate the meat of hens and capons (castrated male chickens), though.

Remember those dovecotes on nobles' estates? Well, the **doves (and sometimes pigeons)** were kept for eating. Sorry, they weren't there just to be cute. They even had a name for the young doves; squabs — these were a delicacy. Their eggs would also be collected. But the feathers were also put to good use (*fluffs pillows, pats mattress*).

This was definitely only for the elite – they were given special permission to keep doves.

Ducks and geese were also included as poultry. Their eggs and meat are delicious. Again, their feathers weren't wasted. Good news: even serfs could enjoy these.

Geese have the added bonus of being very good guard creatures — they honk loudly when anybody approaches and can be heard from a considerable distance. They may even give chase.

Herbs and Spices

Now, at least in monasteries, there were separate herb gardens for culinary use (kitchen) and medicinal (physic).

For now, let us concentrate on the kitchen herbs. Spices were usually purchased. The most commonly used ones for food were:

- Betony
- Cardamom
- Cinnamon
- Clove
- Coriander
- Cubeb (pepper)
- Cumin
- Dill
- Galangal
- Ginger
- Grains of paradise
- Laurel (aka bay leaf)
- Lovage
- Mace
- Meadowsweet
- Mint
- Mustard
- Myrtle
- Nutmeg
- Oregano
- Parsley
- Pepper
- Rosemary
- Rue
- Saffron
- Sage
- Savory
- Thyme

As you can see, there was quite a wide variety. The point is, that food was not bland. Even the serfs may have had ready availability of herbs in their little gardens.

Sugar was extremely expensive, but the nobles made full use of it. **Honey** was a cheaper option and more accessible.

Salt was also a valuable commodity. As I live in Hampshire, I'd like to note that it was commonly harvested from the saltmarshes in Bitterne Manor, along the banks of the River Itchen (amongst a few other places). It was commonly used for curing/preserving meat and fish.

As a condiment, salt was only at the top table. Ergo, people sat "above the salt".

It is reasonable to have a few herbs growing alongside veg in a serf's garden/field/patch. Popular, cheap flavourings included mustard and onions.

Salad

Salad was served but not as we know it. Everyone could enjoy a little starter of salad consisting of herbs, flowers, lettuce/spinach, and onions/leek/garlic/scallions, mixed with a little oil and vinegar. Sometimes, even a little bit of fruit would find its way in. They were really quite medicinal.

Bread

Bread formed a major part of anyone's diet. What changed was the *quality*.

It could be made from wheat, rye, oats or barley.

In perhaps a reversal of our modern thinking, brown bread was eaten by the poor. However, it was roughly milled and quite tough. Whereas the nobility had finely ground, wheat, white flour. The very finest being paindemain, probably from the Latin *panis dominicus* (lordly bread).

Rye bread was eaten in the form of sourdough. It had an earthy, tangy flavour and dense texture.

CAUTION: rye may contain ergot (*Claviceps purpurea fungus*) – may cause painful burning, fever, spasms, hallucinations, paralysis, tremors, gangrene or even death! Look up St Anthony's Fire if you're particularly interested in Ergotism.

Oats were often combined with some wheat flour and honey to make a sweet yet earthy loaf. Because of the addition of wheat flour, it can be assumed this was another option for the wealthy. Modern diners of a certain sandwich chain may know of this yummy, honey oat combination.

The nutty-flavoured **barley** bread was essentially a last resort when harvests were bad. It lacks the gluten required to hold it together well.

In the very worst case, peas, beans, chestnuts or acorns could be used.

But it was also **regional**. The south grew more wheat, so was more commonly eaten there. **Flatbread** was more common in the north and the highlands, where they grew more barley, rye and oats. Flatbread could be baked upon an upturned pot over the embers of the home hearth.

You may see references to **leavened bread**. This was bread which had a rising agent, e.g. yeast (referenced in Late Old English as foam; *gist*). Peasants wanting leavened bread would probably have had to use a lord's communal oven to bake it (for a fee), or buy it from a baker.

In order of finest to poorest, the types of bread were:
- **Paindemain** – white flour which had been sifted two or three times
- **Wastel** – fine, white flour
- **Cocket** – more like a cracker
- **Cheat** – made of wholewheat but with the bran removed
- **Tourte** – brown bread which included the husk
- **Horse** – made of beans or peas
- **Clapbread** – barley or oats

NB Trenchers were probably **not** as common as we've been led to believe. They were supposedly plates made of brown bread baked especially for that purpose. But it was very wasteful as the bread plate wasn't eaten. It would've been more a showy-offy thing at banquets.

Throughout the medieval period, breakfast was often deemed a decadence. The Church frowned upon it. However, one may have a small piece of bread washed down with a little ale, or wine if you were fancy.

To put it into **context**: monks were allotted 1 lb (around 450g) of bread per day. In the UK today, a standard medium sliced loaf is 800g. So, half a loaf or ten slices per day.

Fun fact: bread was so important that it inspired the first English law to regulate the sale and production of food in the 13th century. **The Assize of Bread and Ale** was still in force at the beginning of the 19th century (although it had been amended).

The Assize adjusted the *weight* of bread according to the price of wheat. So, if the price of corn went up, the size of the loaf went down. Similarly, it determined how many gallons of ale could be purchased for a penny.

And there was even a special Loaf Mass (Lammas) conducted in church on 1st August, where the first loaf of the harvest was blessed.

Bread wasn't eaten just in rolls or loaves. Oh, no. Breadcrumbs were a common ingredient in **sauces**, again more for the rich folk. A great thickening agent.

And even in **medicine** e.g. mouldy bread was applied to wounds in poultices to help them heal. Caudle was given to new mothers and the infirm as a restorative, and often contained paindemain flour or breadcrumbs.

Oh, and don't forget the little bread wafers given at **Holy Communion**.

Fun fact: the etymology of the word **lord** has roots in the Anglo-Saxon / Old English word *hlafweard*, meaning one who guards the loaves. **Lady** then comes from *hlaefdige*, meaning bread-kneader. And **servant** comes from *hlafæta*; loaf-eater.

Pottage and Frumenty

Pottage was a dish anyone could enjoy.

The term **pottage** seems to date from the 12th century. Basically, it's vegetables and stock cooked in a pot or cauldron. So, like a stew or broth.

The peasants would have a pot over their range fire where they could chuck in stuff. Popular vegetables included: cabbage, onion, leek, celery and peas. They may have some herbs growing which could be added for flavour: parsley, sage, rosemary or thyme (you're singing now, aren't you?). Some grains may have been included. Occasionally, they may have scraps of meat they could pop in. This would have been a thin broth eaten *with* bread.

Caution: food poisoning has always been known. And said pot would not have been perpetually refilled without ever emptying or cleaning. They weren't dumb!

Whereas the rich people had **frumenty**; a nice thick version. Frumenty was similar to porridge. It was made of cracked wheat boiled in milk. The Latin word *frumentum* from which it gets its name means grain. In fairness, in its simplest form, even peasants could eat frumenty. However, the nobles added eggs, almonds (including the milk), sugar, currants and saffron.

The savoury version of frumenty which used broth instead of milk, and meat such as venison was a popular 'subtlety' dish at banquets.

Dessert

As if all that wasn't enough, there was a dessert course. Because we all know there's always 'dessert tummy' space, even when we say we're full.

Cakes weren't really a thing. There were a few, such as honey cakes. But as there wasn't any self-raising flour, they leaned towards the bready end of the spectrum.

Pastry was huge though. I make mention in my books of apple and blackberry pie; totally a thing. And one of my own favourites (not that you'd tell from the way I write about it. LOL).

Other dishes included plums sweetened in rosewater or pears stewed in honey and wine. Cream custard tarts were available. Cold custards and milky desserts were on offer.

Rose pudding was made by blanching white rose petals and mixing with warm milk and cornflour, cinnamon, sugar, ginger, chopped dates and pine nuts - and cooled.

Banquets

The rich needed to keep up with the Jones'. Big gatherings were a great way of keeping abreast of current affairs and trying to garner influence. Often, these would be in the form of lavish feasts, particularly around important days e.g. Christmas, Easter, weddings or harvest. But the uber rich would hold vast banquets which went to the extreme.

In medieval manor houses, one would expect to find a Great Hall where functions would take place. There would usually be a dais / raised platform for the lord and his most important guests. Then, in descending order of importance, other folk would be seated (on wooden benches at tables). They would only be seated after Mass, though.

Guests may include nobles, the bailiff, officials, farm workers, tenant farmers etc. Depending on who was in attendance, one would want to display the wealth and importance of the household. The more guests, the more food was required, which meant a lot of planning. Beasts would have to be hunted and stored in good order.

The lords *may* have **three courses of fifteen dishes**, each brought in amidst fanfares and entertainments (musicians, tumblers, jugglers, singers and dancers). Soup/pottage, meats, fish and fruits. The meats may include crane, swan, suckling pig or peacock for super fancy events.

A **subtlety** (or sotelty) may be presented as a table decoration between courses too. These were typically made of marchpane (marzipan). And would be carved in ornate ways, depicting figures most likely to please the guests. Other subtleties could include a whole swan or peacock roasted in its feathers.

At the other end of the scale, one may have lowkey, regular dinners for one's local friends and dignitaries. Friars were popular guests as they collected and spread gossip, and one gained brownie points for helping the religious.

Most meals were communal affairs. All the 'household' would eat together. Towards the end of the medieval period, nobles began to dine alone in privacy but were considered snooty for doing so. After all, there was an interdependence between all people, and that was to be honoured.

In short, feasts were a foodie celebration. Banquets were the more extravagant, all-singing, all-dancing affairs.

Fun fact: Brightly coloured food was fashionable – red, yellow and blue would often adorn the table! On May Day, all food was coloured green.

Fast Food

Hail, wanderers from fantasy lands. I suspect your ears are pricking up the most at this – and who can blame you? Characters in fantasy novels are often hurtling across lands on urgent quests, so need to grab food where/when they can.

Even the Ancient Romans had a form of fast food, so it's no real surprise to find ready-to-eat / street food in England from at least the 12th century. Chaucer again, helps us with a rather unflattering description of a cook in *The Canterbury Tales*. According to historical records, York had 35 cookshops alone – the medieval equivalent of McDonalds; the things were sprouting up all over the place!

Cookshops grew in popularity and could mostly be found in busy towns or cities. The poor folk of the town were likely to use them, particularly those who had no cooking facilities at home.

Some cookshops were sited at the city gates whilst others were in the market square. Travellers as much as locals therefore had easy access to delicious (if somewhat dubious) nosh. I mean, there were hygiene regulations, but (*waggles hand*) – these aren't always adhered to even today, is all I'm saying. There were some prosecutions of vendors selling pies containing meat unfit for consumption!

There were options; some had a room you could sit in to feast upon your purchase, whilst others were takeaway only.

Akin to the selling of ale, goodwives could open the doors to their dwelling, stick up a sign and sell their surplus meals, so long as it was cooked i.e. no raw food was allowed.

Typically, one might find **dishes** of roasted meat (usually beef or mutton), fish, stews, rissoles, (beef) ribs, sheep's feet, cheese, pescods (peapods), flans, pastries, wafers and cheesecakes would be available. Onion and mustard would probably be the main flavourings as they were cheap, and they were serving the poor.

And folk could take their own ingredients along to be cooked into a pie or pasty.

Alternatively, there were dedicated **pie shops, bakers** (for bread) and **taverns or alehouses** (for ale). In some places, you could also find **hucksters**; pedlars of bread, vegetables, fish or grain in small quantities, who would shout out their wares.

NB Outside of towns and cities, i.e. the countryside, most folk made their own meals at home.

Let us wander into a **tavern** now. For these are what many writers cherish. Now, think of these as a pub.

By the late Middle Ages, taverns *could* be substantial buildings containing several rooms. Beer and/or wine would be sold. Men and women could frequent them as they were the social hub of the village. Business deals could be made within their walls. In the cold winter months, one would expect a good fire to warm themselves by.

As well as the obvious drinking - gambling, singing and whoring took place in these establishments. And like any good pub on a modern Friday night, they could get raucous and eventually violent. We know this thanks to court records – ooh err.

It's a little unclear as to whether they actually served food, or whether people bought food from a cookshop and ate it in the tavern.

Taverns were subject to the village/town curfew. When that bell rang, folk had to disperse.

Not to be confused with **alehouses**, which I alluded to along with cookshops. So, typically women could open up their home to sell their surplus ale, and close the doors as soon as supplies ran out. A sign would indicate when they were open. Because of this, they were fairly random in occurrence, but were popular everywhere.

I believe, like the cookshop ladies, these private sellers had signs indicating when they were open for business, and some had a room for drinking whilst others did not.

This is where we get 'public house' and therefore '**pub'** from btw.

I'll talk more about **inns** under the travel section. However, these did indeed provide food, beverage and accommodation, more for travellers.

If taverns were more like our pubs, inns were more like a *Premier Inn* or motel. Park up your horse in the stable, store your belongings securely, warm yourself by the fire, revive your wits with a bit of grub and ale or wine before resting your travel-weary head for the night.

NB These were for the rich people.

Dishes

During my research, I've come across many recipes. Some of the dishes I've mentioned in my own books (along with appropriate festivals) include:

- Lamb (roasted) (**Candlemas**)
- **Pancakes. Beef, cheese and ales** (St Valentine/**Shrove Tuesday**)
- *Viaunde Cypre* - a stiffened dish usually made of ground pork, almond milk and spices, but for Lent, it was turned into one of ground crab meat and pomegranates. (**Lent**)
- **Roast lamb** with ginger sauce. **Eggs, simnel loaves & mead (Easter Sunday)**
- *Pourcelet Farci* (suckling pig) with *poivre jaunet* (yellow pepper) sauce (**Whitsun**)
  Served with **Whitsun Ale**
- Fig tart
- *Oystres in Cevey* (**Ember Days** after Whitsun) ~ a rich dish of oysters stewed in a spiced wine sauce
- *Bourbelier de Sanglier* (**St John The Baptist** feast) ~ roast boar with a spiced wine sauce
- Apple and blackberry pie
- Frumenty
- **Rastons** (for **Lammas**) ~ small round loaves made from sweetened bread dough with egg
- *Chireseye* ~ a kind of bread pudding using cherry juice and wine for flavouring, decorated with flowers
- **Tart in Ymbre Day** (for **The Exaltation of the Holy Cross Ember Day**) ~ a sort of onion and cheese quiche with herbs, currants and saffron
- **Caudle** ~ a hot drink of ale, egg yolks, honey, saffron and bread consumed especially after severe illness or childbirth
- Goose (for **Michaelmas and/or All Saints**)
- Apple fritters

- **Eel**, and **soul cakes** (**All Souls**) (*coughs*) Plus bread & some myrtle tea for quelling queasiness after too much cider on All Saints
- **Martlemas beef** (for **Martinmas**) and St Martin's wine
- **Apple muse** – dessert like a stewed apple and bread mush – enjoyed by all ranks
- **Grete Pye** and an **open-arse tart** and **bryndons** (Christmas)

NB 'Open-arse' was a fruit (now called medlar).

The great pye was like a multi-meat pork pie.

And bryndons were small cakes in a sauce of wine, fruit, and nuts.

Incidentally, **when you sign up to my newsletter, you can currently (at the time of publishing) claim your FREE, exclusive copy of** *Recipes From Love Habit*. It contains recipes for many of these dishes. The sign-up form is detailed at the end of this book.

Breakfast, Lunch, Supper

As previously mentioned, breakfast was regarded with somewhat of a sneer.

But I did just want to explain **lunch**. Bear with me, as this can get confusing, and historical accounts debate this. But, to my mind, **the midday meal was what was called 'dinner'**. This would be more likely the time of feasts or main meals because of the amount of daylight. With poor roads, brigands and little light, going anywhere in the evening would have been extremely hazardous. Plus, there were no guest bedrooms yet, so sleepovers were a bit weird.

Therefore, **the evening meal was their supper**. And a light one at that.

Of course, if you were working hard all day, you may have a more substantial breakfast and scoff down a big meal at whatever ungodly hour you got back home.

Just know that the "Ploughman's Lunch" was a 20th century advertising creation. Although, people in the fields may well have eaten bread, cheese, perhaps an onion with beer or cider in the Middle Ages.

Drink

Water is subject to debate. Yes, a lot of it was polluted; everything went into rivers. However, **wells** were a thing. And there were a few water supply systems, such as *The Conduit* in London, which ran fresh spring water through lead pipes into the city.

Ale (not beer!) was common. Although, to be drunk as much as some people suggest, England would not have had enough grain to supply that demand. But it is known that housewives brewed ale and sold the surplus form their own premises (ale houses). And monks were very good at brewing too.

The flavour of medieval ale would have been sweet, fruity, earthy, spicy and herby but with a bitter finish. The alcohol content varied; the first brew was the strongest. The mash would then be used for a second time to produce a medium strength result. And lastly, the third one would create **small ale** which had the lowest alcohol content but the most bitter taste.

Ale was bought from alehouses in pints i.e. when not bought in bulk.

Posset Ale - was warmed milk mixed with ale (or wine) and was often spiced. The addition of egg yolks seems to have been optional. But it appears to have been a forerunner of eggnog. It was enjoyed as a sleep aid and to cure colds and indigestion. It was even considered an aphrodisiac. It does sound very comforting.

NB Hops weren't cultivated in England until about 1520 — the stuff that makes beer as opposed to ale.

Cider was originally brought to us by the Romans. Medieval monks then became the main cider producers. There's a common theme here! Mind you, when one's life is spent in quiet devotion at all hours of the day and night, one can hardly blame them for enjoying a tipple.

Back in 1204, a manor house in Runham, Norfolk, is recorded as the first time someone was *paid* in cider. The idea soon caught on, and farm labourers could be 'paid' eight pints of cider per day. Nice! (*hiccup*).

There are two main types of English cider; the West Country and the Kent/East Anglia. The latter uses almost exclusively dessert/culinary apples, so tends to be clearer and lighter. Whereas the West Country folk use more cider apples which are sharper (ooh arr!).

Apples, historically, grew better than grapes in England, so, y'know, convenience.

Wine was a popular choice for the wealthy. And it was viewed as being medicinal - huzzah!

Annual purchases of wine could be:

- ❖ 3 ½ pipes of red wine (1 pipe = 105 imperial gallons)
- ❖ 2 hogsheads of white wine (1 hogshead = approx. 52 imperial gallons)

White wine would go off quicker, so red was more popular.

Mulled wine - hot, spiced wine - very tasty stuff!

Hypocras / Hippocras was a specific medicinal, spiced wine. Named after the Ancient Greek physician, Hippocrates. I made my own version; it's *very* sweet: lotta sugar!

There are many different recipes, but most contain: wine obviously (red or white), cinnamon, cardamom, cloves, nutmeg, galangal, ginger and sugar.

It's actually cold brewed for a day usually (as opposed to warmed, mulled wine). Supposedly, it does wonders for the digestion. And therefore, it became the closing part of banquet menus. It was also seen as a moist, warming aid for ailments of the chest, lungs and stomach.

I'd also like to mention **wassail**. Heated cider, laced with spices such as cloves, cinnamon and ginger. Traditionally drunk as part of Christmas festivities.

To 'go wassailing' is to gather in the orchards, sprinkling this hot cider around the trees to protect them from evil spirits. It became a thing for Twelfth Night (the end of Christmastide). This then evolved into a practice where people would go door-to-door, singing in return for a cup of wassail. This could get drunkenly violent!

Mead was a form of honey wine but had become less common. A fermented drink made of water, honey and yeast. Spices (such as cloves) and herbs may be added.

Table Manners

Whilst we're talking about food, please may I say something frightfully important? **Table manners were a thing**! Do not fall prey to the films which show people gnawing on great big turkey legs (*shudders*).

Grace would be said before every meal by the chaplain. Religion was ever present.

Outside the Great Hall, you would find a laver; a small basin for washing your hands before and after meals. And there were finger bowls shared between two people on the tables.

The lady of the house would pile her plate high and distribute food to those on her right and left, and anyone else she wished to reward for good behaviour.

Every person would have their own knife, attached to their belt. **No forks**! People were expected to elegantly slice meat with their knife and take it to their mouth with their fingers. Chewing with their mouth closed (much to the relief of this misophonia sufferer!).

Spoons were used for soups, stews and frumenty - which could be served hot or cold, either first or last course.

Napkins in medieval England were pieces of cloth. If one was of higher rank, this would be draped over one's left shoulder. Lower ranks, over their arm.

If someone of higher rank entered or left the room, the lower orders would stand.

Belching and over-stuffing one's mouth were big no-nos. And nobody should ever pick their teeth with their knife.

The upper crust of the bread should be sliced and offered to the highest-ranking people. Ah, that's where "the upper crust" comes from!

Writing Prompt – Food

Your character sits down to their main meal of the day. Where are they and what time is it? Is it light outside? What's on the menu?

- Does your MC eat meat at all?
- What vegetables do they have?
- How good was their daily bread?
- Do religious observances control their diet?
- Do they eat out?
- What do they drink?

FARMING

Farming was not just a way of life in the Middle Ages — it WAS life. If crops failed, the community would starve.

And there were indeed periods of **famine**. Focusing on 15th century England, there were deficient harvests 1400-03, 1408-10, 1416-17, and 1428-29. This then reached famine status 1437-39; the worst of the 15th century.

For most of human history, the vast majority of folk would have been involved in one way or another in agriculture. People would live in settlements, each supporting one another even indirectly e.g. tools supplied by the blacksmith were used in farming.

I believe the percentage of the working populace in England in the 15th century who worked directly in agriculture was around 60%.

Farming Calendar

It's useful to know this when looking at medieval England, as it affects what people were doing:

Month	Jobs
January	~ Mending and making tools, repairing fences, planting, weaving
February	~ Ploughing and fertilising
March	~ Sowing, weeding, ploughing
April	~ Pruning, weeding, harrowing, scaring birds
May	~ Digging ditches, first ploughing of fallow fields, scaring birds, weeding
June	~ Haymaking, second ploughing of fallow field, sheep-shearing
July	~ Ploughing, gathering
August	~ Harvesting, tying, winnowing
September	~ Harvesting, tying, winnowing, milling
October	~ Sowing, milling, weaving
November	~ Butchering, smoking/salting, weaving
December	~ Mending and making tools, collecting, digging

The Farming Year

Let's look at farming in more detail.

Michaelmas (29 September)

The cycle begins! Crops were sown. Winter crops (wheat and rye) were ploughed. The aim was to complete this by All Saints Day (1st November) when the harvest reeve and some workers may well be expected to dine at The House.

As the bread grains were sown, the previous summer's crop had to be threshed and winnowed.

Autumn/Winter Months

After the harvest, fields would be ploughed (the final ploughing of the year).

Plough beasts were fattened and the ploughs and carts would be repaired, often by travelling carpenters.

General tools and fences would be made/repaired through to February.

Withies (willow rods) would be harvested once the leaves had dropped, ready to be weaved into baskets.

Older fruit trees would be pruned.

In November, if a farm had pigs, acorns would be collected to feed them.

And in November/December, animals would be butchered. Some of the 'flesh' (meat) would be smoked or salted to ensure it lasted all winter. Peasants would kill their own animals.

Monday Plough would be celebrated on the first Monday after the Eve of Epiphany/Twelfth Night (05 January), when agricultural work would restart after the Christmastide break.

Candlemas (02 February)

Spring ploughing would begin. Depending on hard frosts, it could be delayed up until late April.

Once this was completed, a celebration may well take place with an attending minstrel and some special food such as garfish, sole or plaice.

Spring

In March, stable dung and guano from dovecotes would be spread over the fields. Horse, oxen, pig and even human droppings could be used as fertiliser.

Ploughmen had their own fields to attend to as well as the fallow fields.

March – April was lambing season for those farms with sheep.

Spring sowing of barley, oats, legumes and vetches would be carried out in April. Peasants would also plant vegetables in their own gardens late winter/early spring. And there was harrowing to be done.

In April/May, fruit trees (apples, pears and sometimes berry bushes) may be planted in the orchards and/or the peasants gardens.

In sun or showers, people would dig ditches and begin ploughing the farrow fields in May.

Cows would start giving milk fully as they ate the fresh spring pasture.

Human scarecrows would leap around to scare off birds until the seeds sprouted. Children as young as three could run about the fields, banging drums or sticks, ringing bells, clapping and/or shouting.

Then the corn fields would get weeded – men, women and children would get involved in this.

June

By June, ploughs would be in need of repairs.

The second ploughing of the farrow field would be done.

Sheep shearing would be carried out, followed by a feast.

And hay would be made (whilst the sun shines, as the saying goes). This could be done in June/July, and was vital as it would feed the animals over winter.

Crops would be weeded in July.

This was actually the **leanest time of year**; supplies would be low and the new harvests had not yet come in. (*shudders*) All that work on an empty belly!

Lammas (01 August)

The wheat harvest would hopefully be ready. This was the husbandry and spiritual feast. The first harvest would be consecrated as a Eucharist offering (in Loaf Mass/Lammas).

Tenants, neighbours, local farmers and boon workers (those obliged to as part of their rental contract) would all help out.

As men cut the crops, women would tie them into sheaves for the carter to load and transport to the barn for storage.

The household would bake bread and brew ale every 2-3 days instead to the usual 5-6 to ensure all were well fed.

Harvest could take around 28 days to complete – a celebration was definitely in order after all that! Especially as this was the basis for their survival. **Grain** may have accounted for around 80% of a person's calorie intake; think bread, ale and pottage.

Threshing – separating the grain from the stalks, was done by men hitting the stalks with a flail.

Winnowing (separating the grain from the chaff; the outer casing) would ensue. Often, they would sieve the wheat heads, letting the chaff blow away in the breeze (or encouraged with the wafting of a sheet).

Threshing and winnowing could take up to two months. During which time, the **miller** would start grinding the grain into flour. Water mills were popular as they weren't weather dependant, so long as there was a stream nearby of course. But windmills were also in use.

Also, in late summer/August, fruit would be picked from hedgerows and trees.

Peas, beans and vetches would be harvested. Much of this would be dried for winter use.

September

In early September, young fruit trees would be pruned.

This was about a month before Michaelmas, when it would all begin again.

Types of Farming

Wool was a big deal. It was a growth economy in the 1500s. So, of course, there was **sheep farming**. One of the huge benefits was the lower maintenance cost of around £2 per annum; 10s for each shepherd's wage, and under £1 for essentials such as fencing, grease and tar. Sheep themselves cost 1s to purchase or even just 1d (a penny) for a lamb.

The job of a **shepherd** was lowly but thanks to its affinity with Christian ideology, it carried a slightly higher status than other farm labourer roles. He was expected to be a kindly type (a bit simple) as sheep would shun him if he wasn't a gentle chap, apparently — this was generally accepted advice at the time, don't blame me.

Cattle were also kept, more for milking. Incidentally, very few people seem to have drunk milk; it was used more for butter, desserts and cheese. Cows were expensive, though; 10s each as opposed to 1s for a sheep. And they ate more. But then one could tan hides and sell the leather for horses' tack or to repair carts etc.

One of the biggest impacts on the English countryside was **arable farming** (crops). Although the cost of this started climbing thanks to the raising of wages and the scarcity of labour.

Other costs could include things such as: ploughing, sowing, reaping, carting, capital investment in a stock of plough beasts (& maintenance thereof), repairs to ploughs, purchase of seed, wages and the cost of the harvest feast (which could be lavish indeed – more than the cost of the harvest itself!).

The ensuing hay would also help feed the livestock over winter.

Measuring the Land

Land distribution estimates suggest that the English nobility owned 20% of English lands, the Church and Crown 33%, the gentry 25%, with the remainder (22%) owned by peasant farmers.

All this land had to be measured.

Alright, this gets a bit complex. I'm including it for information only. Clarification in case you come across these terms and wonder what they mean. Please don't worry – you're unlikely to have to know it to this degree. And I'm not going to be handing out a test on it, or anything.

Acres were one form of measurement; the strip of land that could be ploughed in one day by a team of oxen pulling a plough. Presuming one had a team of 8 oxen.

NB Acres weren't standardised until 1878.

A **rood** was ¼ of an acre (approx. 5.5 yards). And each rood could be made up of 40 **perches**.

But acres could also be divided into **furlongs**; the long furrow/strip one could plough before turning. For comparison, there are around 8 furlongs in a mile.

A throwback to the Saxons was a **hide**. This was the amount of land one family could live on, and was approx. 120 acres aka a carucate (depending on location and quality of land). This becomes relevant as when the country was divided into **shires**, each shire was made up of 100 hides, so was called a **hundred** — this is a term you may come across in taxation/land registry/general research/law.

Don't get scared/overwhelmed. If your character is just passing, it's completely acceptable to just say that they passed **fields**. The measurements only come into force if your people are going to mention land disputes, tithes or are farming the land in any great detail.

Working the Land

The **manor** was a term for the whole estate. It was effectively a small village, with maybe as little as 100 acres under its remit. The nobility may own several manors and may have to travel between them throughout the year – they weren't necessarily close to one another. The **lord** of the manor lived in the manor house.

They were responsible for the community who lived on their lands. The **serfs** would have their own dwellings and were usually given a section of land so they could grow vegetables etc. for their family's use. There may also have been communal land included for grazing or wood gathering.

Serfs would farm the lord's land maybe three days per week, and their own on the other days. Unless it was harvest time; in which case it was all hands to the fields until it was all collected.

There would usually be a small **river** or stream running through the estate – water being a necessity to life.

An area of **woodland** was also essential. You may come across the term **'coppice'** or 'copse' — an area of woodland/forest/grove where young trees or shrubs are periodically cut back to near ground level (felling) to stimulate growth and provide firewood or timber. A form of forest management which dates back to the Stone Age.

Other buildings on the estate/manor would include a church, mill and barns. If you've ever played those computer games where you have to build a community/civilisation, you'll get the idea. What are the basic needs of humans to survive?

If you hear tell of a **demesne** (aka domain), this was the area of land reserved exclusively for the landowner, and was typically around 35-40% of the estate's land.

Working that land took a lot of labour.

Most places employed **the three field system** – One field was planted in the autumn, one in spring, whilst the third was left **fallow** (unused; giving it time to recover). The fields would be in rotation from year to year.

You may hear of '**land enclosure**'. It began in the 12th century. Basically, it was a division or consolidation of communal fields, meadows, pastures, and other arable lands. Land was enclosed by way of erecting fences/hedges around, thus preventing common grazing, the collection of firewood or turf (for fuel) (*boo!*).

The boundaries of this land were highly disputed in the manorial courts and deep-set resentment rumbled on for many years.

Maybe you've heard of places such as Clapham Common. Yes, this was common land. And the occupier of such a plot of land would be a **commoner**.

The New Forest in Hampshire still retains commoner's rights from the Anglo-Saxon period, such as: Pasture, Mast, Marl, Turbary, Sheep and Fuelwood.

e.g. Each year, from Sep-Nov, pigs are turned out for pannage (foraging for fallen acorns).

You will also find ponies, donkeys and cows grazing throughout the year, just roaming around quite happily across the national park, even in the roads. Cattle grids keep them within the boundaries.

It's actually a fascinating heritage area which maintains old-fashioned rural life, handed down through families across the centuries. Worth a look into if you're ever curious.

Granges

A monastic grange was a farm owned and run by a monastic community. The idea was to provide food and materials for the monastery, and they would sell surplus for a small profit. They first started to appear in the 12th century and continued to be in use until the Dissolution.

Writing Prompt - Farming

There are people working the fields - is your character viewing them or are they one of them?

- Is your MC expected to help with the harvest?
- Do they generally help farm the land?
- If so, what farming activities are they up to?
- Is there a convenient barn to sneak behind for a quick kiss & cuddle?

WILDLIFE

This will be a very brief section. However, it is important to know which animals your characters might encounter. The reading community were up in arms when one book mentioned gophers in a book set in England. And I'm here to provide information for a realistic book, so am duty bound to offer some details.

So, in medieval England, we commonly had:
- Badgers – look cute and are good for the ecosystem
- Beavers – help reduce flood risk
- Birds of prey e.g red kites, common buzzards and white-tailed eagles
- Deer
- Feral cats
- Foxes
- Great bustard – a large, flightless bird (now extinct)
- Hedgehogs – eat slugs and snails
- Owls – bad omens
- Pigeons – popular in pies
- Pine martens – of the weasel family, cat-sized, eat birds
- Porpoises – apparently were caught on our shores for food
- Rats and mice – extremely prevalent
- Shrews – like a small mole (which also existed, formerly known as moldwarps; 'earth throwers')
- Skylarks – little birds which sang beautifully but were also caught for the table
- Squirrels
- Voles – a mole-sized, herbivore rodent
- Weasels – good pest control; eat voles and mice

NB Wolves had pretty much been eradicated by the end of the medieval era. But had been in steep decline since the 12th century.

And bears haven't been since around the start of the 6th century.

Writing Prompt – Wildlife

A creature cries out…in the night?

- Does your MC see/hear any wildlife?
- Are any good/bad omens to be gleaned from that?
- Or do they hunt any animals (see the Law section for restrictions, and the Sport section under Pasttimes for details on falconry/hunting)?

MEDICINE AND DISEASE

CAUTION: Some of this is going to get a bit graphic.

Crumbs, where do we start? Maybe the attitudes towards medicine.

General approaches to patients included: examination of pulse, urine, stool, and blood. Treatments included bathing, bloodletting, diet, praying, purging, astrology and herbalism.

Medical Texts

There were medical texts which contained a wealth of information. Galen seems to be the most frequently mentioned, but here's a list of the popular reference materials medieval medical folk referred to:

- **Pseudo-Apuleius Herbarius** / Herbarium Apuleii (possibly by Apuleius of Madaura) (c. 150BC) – later translated into the Old English, Herbarium
- **Rhizotomica by Crateuas**, (a 3 volume herbal text) (c. 100BC)
- **Regimen Sanitatis Salernitanum** (c. 1100-1200) (a didactic poem on health and medicine)
- **De Materia Medica** by Dioscorides (Greek; c50AD) (incl. herbalism from Middle East & Asia)
- **Naturalis Historia** / The Natural History by Pilny The Elder (77AD)
- **The Galenic Corpus** (the collection of writings of Galen, c165AD)
- **Bald's Leechbook** (Saxon) (written in about 900–950AD)
- **Trotula** (Group of three texts on women's medicine composed in Salerno, Italy, in the 12th century)
- **Causae et Curae** by Hildegard of Bingen (12th century) – Hildegard was a German abbess and an extraordinary woman.

A Brief History of Medicine

- **4000 BC** - Origins of Ayurveda
- **2600 BC** - Imhotep – Ancient Egypt's priest-physician (later deified as a god of medicine)
- **1800 BC** - Kahun Gynaecological Papyrus
- **700 BC** - Knidos medical school (and one at Cos), Greece
- **500-300 BC** - Hippocrates (of Cos) wrote the first Hippocratic oath. It's still in use today, although somewhat different to back then. However, "do no harm" still lies at its heart.
- **129-216 BC** - Galen – Greek physician, surgeon and scholar of the Roman Empire, whose findings formed a complete medical philosophy which dominated medicine throughout the Middle Ages until the beginning of the modern era
- **1030** - Avicenna - The Canon of Medicine - remained a standard textbook in Muslim and European universities until the 18th century
- **1084** - first documented hospital in England, in Canterbury
- **1100-1300** - medical schools were founded in Europe; Bologna, Montpellier, Oxford, Paris and Salerno
- **1249** - Roger Bacon writes about convex lens spectacles for treating long-sightedness
- **1260** - Louis IX established Les Quinze-Vingts in Paris; originally a retreat for the blind, it became a hospital for eye diseases and is now one of the global pioneers in its field

Life Expectancy

Throughout the medieval era (and even up until the Regency), the average life expectancy was around thirty-five years old, across much of Europe.

Now, it is important to factor in the exceptionally **high infant mortality rate**.

If you reached your twentieth birthday, you'd be likely to see your fiftieth And probably even your sixty-ninth. It's possible many lived into their 70s or 80s.

So, no, not everybody died young.

The Humors

Medical thinking at the time sought to temper the four humors of the body:

1. **Sanguine** (Blood) – linked with air and spring. As a personality; optimistic and active.
2. **Choleric** (Yellow Bile) - fire and summer. Short-tempered and irritable.
3. **Melancholic** (Black Bile) – earth and autumn. Introspective and thoughtful.
4. **Phlegmatic** (Phlegm) – water and winter. Relaxed and peaceful.

These were represented by the four elements, and manifested in the body as hot, cold, dry and moist in any combination thereof. To bring one back into balance, you'd issue a remedy of its opposite e.g. make hot cold.

These could be interrupted by, yes, disease, but also demons, gods, witchcraft and astronomical events.

Hippocrates came up with this theory, but Galen modified it.

It's actually fascinating, but incredibly complex, so I'll leave it at this high-level explanation.

I have actually read a really cool modern book which uses the humors effectively like character traits; *The Four Temperaments* by Randy Rolfe.

Medicinal Herbs

Wise women had known for centuries of the healing properties of plants. And even monks, who administered medical remedies as charity, grew physik/physic gardens. The monks studied and experimented with these herbs and wrote books of their findings.

Everyday folk would visit the monastery, local herbalist, or apothecary to obtain any healing herbs they didn't grow themselves. Chiefly:

- Angelica
- Betony
- Comfrey
- Coriander
- Dandelion
- Elecampane
- English Lavender
- Lovage
- Mallow
- Marjoram
- Myrtle
- Pennyroyal (mint)
- Peppermint
- Rosemary
- Sage
- St. John's Wort
- Thyme
- Vervain
- Wormwood (aka mugwort)
- Yarrow

Sadly, some of the plants were, in fact, toxic, so hindered rather than cured. However, many remedies were effective.

I don't want to bore you with the rundown of all of these. But I did want to give examples of three main herbs, to show how versatile they were. **These are for information and not to be inferred as recommendations.**

Mints

There was an array of mints, and the great medical texts recommended them for various ailments, including:

- **Pennyroyal** – antispasmodic, abortifacient, anti-depressant, anti-inflammatory, bronchodilator, diuretic, expectorant, insect repellent, local anaesthetic, stimulate menses (menstruation), tonsilitis, treatment of snake/scorpion bites
- **Peppermint** – anti-emetic, digestion
- **Spearmint** – antiparasitic, digestion, diuretic
- **Watermint** – digestion, female hygiene, reduce libido, spermicide

Rosemary

Rosemary was one of the most widely used as it was considered a bit of a cure-all. It's a member of the mint family. The flowers, leaves and stems were variously used:

- **Flowers boiled in water** – "use it against all illnesses within the body" as a drink
- **Leaf boiled in white wine** – "make your face white and beautiful, and the hair beautiful."
- **Leaf powdered** – "to bind the arm to help it heal quickly."
- **Flower paste** – "moisten a green cloth, and brush your teeth, and it will kill worms, and protect you from all ills."
- **Root burned on hot coals** (smoke inhalation) – "will cause all rheum to go away."
- **Root boiled in strong vinegar** – "wash your feet in it, and it will make them firm and strong."
- **Leaves** – "put it in your bed, and you will not have nightmares."
- **Cuttings** – "keep it in your house, and you will have nothing to fear from serpents or scorpions."
- **Wood** put in a barrel/cask of wine – "good for every illness, and will drive away boils of the breast."

Other uses included: driving away rage, increasing appetite, to draw diarrhoea from the body, reducing inflammation from gout, restoring sanity, quenching thirst, a worm repellent (from clothing and books).

Sage

The *Regimen Sanitatis Salernitanum* (c. 1100-1200), declares, "Why should a man die in whose garden grows sage?"

Indeed, one of the many names given to sage is *Salvia salvatrix*, meaning 'sage the saviour'. The ancients knew of the great healing properties of this humble herb. But in limited amounts for too much sage actually causes problems.

During times of plague, one could drink the juice of sage with vinegar. But general mouthwashes and gargles used sage with other ingredients.

Sage could be used: against stitch, as a diuretic, to boost memory, cleanse the body of venom/pestilence, lessen phlegm, promote skin healing, reduce menopausal hot flushes, reduce palsy/paralysis/cramp, reduce pain of coming wind, relieve sore throat/tonsilitis, reduce cold sores, reduce fever, treat dysentery, warm cold joints and whiten teeth.

Dioscorides even says the water can be boiled to dye the hair black. However, *The Tacuinum Sanitatis*, says it may *remove* the dark colour from hair. I dunno, I'm not about to try it.

Types of Medical Practitioner

- Physician
- Apothecary
- Barber surgeon
- Wise women
- Midwives

Leech was a general term for doctor/physician. Hence the aforementioned Leechbook btw – it was a medical text, *not* about the blood-sucking things. It means 'to heal' in Old English.

The **physician** was a man who had studied at university for seven to ten years. As many of them were from the clergy, they were not permitted to touch blood. They were more like our modern GP; they would examine and diagnose, but charged high fees.

One would then need to visit the **apothecary** to purchase the recommended remedy; the forerunner to our modern day pharmacy. They would have their own garden of herbs. And they concocted all manner of remedies from herbs, minerals, and animal meats/fats/innards/skins.

Barber surgeons (*wince*) indeed performed both roles; they could cut hair, but also veins. The blood-red and bandage-white poles still visible today, represented that. They might set broken bones, pull teeth or perform amputations (before anaesthetic had been invented!). They were mostly untrained and unhygienic. But they were cheaper than the above options.

Wise women – women who were wise! LOL. But they were. Like the monks, they understood the healing power of herbs. And might even be able to perform minor surgeries.

Midwives will get a special section under feminine hygiene and care in a moment.

Medical Institutions

Within the monasteries, there was an infirmary with a dedicated infirmarer. These seemed to have served their own community more than that of outsiders.

But monks did create **hospitals** from donations received — an estimated 500-1,000 of them. Overseen by the bishop, the monks/canons/nuns provided free healthcare to the locals and pilgrims. Different buildings housed patients with different ailments. They were kept very clean (it's next to Godliness!), and they gave the sick nutritious food.

The religious did tend to view disease as punishment from God, though. So, you'd likely get a good praying over as much as actual physical remedies.

Fun fact: St Bartholemew's Hospital in London (affectionately known as St Barts) was founded in 1123, somehow survived The Dissolution and still helps people today. Huzzah!

From the 12th century, **schools of surgery** were introduced.

The medical surgeon was instructed on **air, diet, exercise and drugs**. The wise ones treated the wounds with vinegar or alcohol. But they were fairly rare, as they were held liable for any fatality which resulted. And there were quite a few mishaps without antibiotics etc.

However, these surgeons performed rapid amputations for those injured in battle - the quicker the better for the patient, to stop the loss of blood. And they made a rudimentary cast for broken limbs too.

First Aid

You could always try to treat minor ailments and diseases yourself. Which, let's face it, you'd try.

For this, you would need a store of: willow bark, honey, cobwebs, moss and live snails. I kid you not. Look:

- **Willowbark** was a painkiller and may even have helped reduce inflammation. Worth giving it a chew, especially if you had a fever or headache! Later inspired aspirin (around 1897).

- **Honey** was readily available. Its stickiness helped bind wounds whilst stopping them from drying out. Turns out, it has antimicrobial properties too, so not as silly as it first sounds. And is making a comeback.

- Now, **cobwebs** are astonishing. I sniffed at the thought, because eww! But, if it was clean, then the sticky web may have actually helped wounds. They would bind them together, and actually contain antiseptic and antifungal properties. The vitamin K in them may help blood clotting too - well, I never!

- Isabel in my book, *Love in the Roses*, has recourse to use **blood moss**. This is used to soak up her menstrual flow. This actually happened! Its technical term is sphagnum moss, and was used for that and also to mop up blood from wounds.

- **Snails** would be used to treat minor cuts and burns. It's been discovered that their slime does indeed contain antiseptic, anaesthetic, antibiotic, antiviral properties, along with collagen and elastin. So good is this icky substance, that it's now being put back into cosmetics.

Vinegar was often used to clean wounds, by the way.

So, there you have it, some helpful and not-so-helpful remedies.

Incidentally, the number of fatalities after medical intervention are in similar proportions today, just before you dismiss it all!

Diseases

Common diseases in the Middle Ages included dysentery ('the flux'), tuberculosis and 'sweating sickness'. Syphilis was rife (aka 'pox', 'great pox' or 'French pox') – not to be confused with smallpox.

The Black Death (aka The Great Pestilence or Bubonic Plague) had been and gone by the 15th century. It occurred, as previously stated, 1348-9 and 1361-2. But the effects were still being felt from the reduced population. I know I'm harping on about that, but it's important.

Yay, the disease was over. But the paranoia lingered as sadly, **there were other general plagues and agues**. Want a closer look at some? Sure you do. It'll be ^fun^!

Dysentery aka The Flux

Dysentery is an inflammation of the large intestine characterized by loose stools containing blood and mucus, and by tenesmus - painful and unproductive attempts to defecate.

Depending on the severity, rapid weight loss can occur. Stomach cramps, dehydration, bloody diarrhoea and abdominal pain are common.

Symptoms last for up to a week, normally.

Medieval treatments included reciting Psalm 56 three times and the 'Our Father' nine times. Also, bloodletting, fasting and resting. Opium could be prescribed. But many approaches were tried: salves, baths, smokes, food and drink, herbal infusions, charms, laxatives and purgatives, powders, and syrups.

Plantain, yarrow and mint seem to have been popular ingredients in herbal remedies. As well as parsley, fenugreek and mugwort which actually are antispasmodic and anti-inflammatory. Egg whites were another ingredient which may have helped as an antimicrobial.

Dysentery was particularly virulent in areas of dense population with poor sanitation and hygiene.

It could be fatal. King John is thought to have died of dysentery in 1216, as did King Edward I in 1307 and King Henry V in 1422. When monarchs die of a disease, it's obviously thought to be a huge problem. And indeed, dysentery was a very real threat to the lives of the populace.

Tuberculosis aka phthisis, the "white plague," or consumption

Yet another ancient infectious disease, possibly going back to the Neolithic period. And our old friend, Hippocrates, also mentions it in his writings, *"a cold humor dripped from the head into the lungs"*.

It was a wasting disease with destruction of the lungs. And was almost always fatal – around 80% mortality rate.

Symptoms included: coughing, cold extremities, fatigue, fever with rigors, sweating, weight loss, pale skin and sunken eyes. It was a slow, melancholy decline in health. Galen wrote of the tell-tale, *"blood stained sputum."*

It particularly struck people between the ages of 18-35, and spread from close contact, particularly in overcrowded areas. It could last several months!

Treatments included bloodletting, expectorants and purgatives, fresh air, healthful diet, exercise e.g. vigorous horse riding and opium.

Some of the more adventurous remedies included eating wolf livers and drinking elephant urine – hard to come by in 15th century England, though. However, one could try butter boiled with honey – far more palatable and available.

Sweating Sickness

In 1485, at the start of the Tudors, there was a rather nasty Sweating Sickness aka English Sweat. It claimed thousands of lives in the 15th and 16th centuries. Part of the horror was its rapid killing power.

It was really rather curious. People remarked, "*...on the special susceptibility of the fair-haired races of Europe for contracting Sweating Sickness*". In fact, it became known as "The English Sweat". It seemed to target particularly the wealthy young men, including students at Oxford and Cambridge.

A person could be absolutely fine, then get a sudden headache and great thirst, and be dead within three to eight hours! But, if the patient survived the first twenty-four hours, they were likely to make a full recovery. Brutal! The average mortality rate is thought to be between 30% to 50%, but it varied greatly.

Each epidemic lasted a matter of weeks. In later outbreaks, monks were greatly affected.

It was unfortunate timing. The first time Sweating Sickness struck was at the very start of the Henry VII's reign, and so his opponents began to say it was punishment from God upon his supporters. It occurred September to October 1485, and killed several thousand.

In reality, we still don't really know what caused this disease or what it was.

Treatment? Oh, obviously, go to bed and don't eat or drink anything. Pile on more blankets and close the windows. Eurgh! Can you imagine? "Oh, thanks, yes, I needed to be made even hotter and not replenish my fluids!?".

Syphilis

Actually, you may not have to worry about this one too much. It really erupted from the very end of the 15th century, but it's good to be aware of it.

By 1495, syphilis had become an epidemic in Europe. At first, it was believed to be another pox. In fact, prior to the 15th century, cases seem to have been misdiagnosed as leprosy. Oops!

Rich and poor alike suffered from this sexually transmitted disease (STD).

Symptoms started with painless ulcers on the genitals a few weeks after sexual contact with an infected person. Then a rash would spread to other parts of the body, accompanied by fatigue, fever and headaches. Large, stinking pustules may then emerge. Aching muscles and bones grew steadily more painful. All these symptoms could then disappear – yay, cured! Nope. The disease merely lay dormant for years.

On the second occurrence, the large pustules would reappear, but bones and flesh would start to degrade too. The nasal cavities may be affected, making sufferers appear as if they had no nose. Lips and eyes might be likewise destroyed. Lastly, the brain and nervous system were affected, sending many folk to the asylum. Did I mention blindness may also occur? We're talking of an extremely unpleasant illness here.

Apologies, but in England, it became known as the French Pox. But each country accused another, quite frankly. It wasn't actually called syphilis until 1530, when am epic poem came out about it. Incidentally, the severity of symptoms started to lessen around that time.

Treatments involved mercury, so if the disease didn't kill you, mercury poisoning might!?

Smallpox

This terrible disease was responsible for more deaths than any other single infectious disease, even plague and cholera. On average, 3 out of 10 people who got it died.

Usually identified by the hard, blistering rash which formed on the skin, smallpox was an infectious disease, spread from person to person (close contact). Other symptoms included: high fever, severe headache, backache, stomach pain and vomiting. It started with sores on the tongue and inside the mouth.

It could last for 2-4 weeks.

Those who survived were often left with scarring, blindness and possibly arthritis.

It was also perhaps one of the oldest diseases in the world, thought to have existed for 3,000 years before its eradication in 1978.

Thanks to the 13th century royal physician, John of Gaddesden, one recommendation for sufferers was to surround them with scarlet (red) cloth and decoration, and feed them red food and drink. This was still in practice in the 16th century! What??

NB Leprosy had all but died out by the end of the 14th century (around 1350), having risen in the 4th century and peaked around the 11th century. So, that's good news.

Common complaints (not diseases) included: gout, constipation and flatulence. Remedies for these to follow.

Remedies

General Terms:

- **Infusion**: pouring hot water over the herb to extract the healing ingredients
- **Decoction**: creating an extract of the herb by boiling it
- **Compress**: a folded cloth moistened with an infusion and applied to the skin
- **Poultice**: an ointment smeared onto a cloth and applied, often hot, to the skin
- **Unguents**: clear, soft, spreadable mixtures applied to the affected area
- **Ointments**: like an unguent, only thicker
- **Lozenges/Pastilles:** hard, solid tablets made from sugar and edible gum mixed with medicinal ingredients/herbs and water. Pressed into shapes and dried under heat. Taken orally.

Bloodletting was performed in cases of fever, as clearly there was too much blood (heat) in the body. And also in cases of plague, smallpox and typhoid.

And it was actually quite a complicated science (*points index finger skyward*).

Astrological calendars and almanacs were consulted. e.g. one should avoid bloodletting when the moon was in the sign of the zodiac governing the part of the body to be bled.

There were diagrams such as "vein man" and "zodiac man" which helped guide the practitioner. Because it wasn't just the arm vein which could be opened. Oh no, there were several locations, such as the armpit or groin depending on the zodiac and ailment.

At one point, at least, Cistercian monks underwent bloodletting four times per year as a preventative measure. It's thought that all monks underwent periodical bloodletting. BUT in 1163, Pope Alexander III issued an edict which banned monks and priests from performing the procedure, declaring it to be barbaric. To be fair, this does seem quite an ordeal as monks had to rest in the infirmary for up to three days following. So, it's probably best that it was stopped.

However, the general practice does seem to have yielded positive results. After all, it was performed for thousands of years. It's thought to have started in Ancient Egypt. And didn't stop until the late 19th century.

Leeches (of the wormy kind) were indeed used as another form of bloodletting. It was seen as less invasive and more natural. Nom nom nom!

Sweating was a way of ridding the body of excess fluid - fires, piles of blankets, hot cloths...all could be applied to encourage sweat.

Inducing vomiting or issuing a laxative were also deemed fine ways of ridding the body of those nasty excess humours.

It was Galen who seems to have first suggested packing purulent (puss-secreting) wounds with **mouldy bread**. I briefly mentioned this whilst discussing bread earlier. But you know what? Some people class this as the first (incidental) penicillin. He may not have known why, but he certainly knew it helped. At some point during the medieval era, someone seems to have thought it a good idea to mix sheep droppings and other things in with this. I think I'll just take the mouldy bready, thanks!

For **major wounds**, cauterization was a last resort — the burning of the skin with a heated instrument or caustic substance. It was incredibly painful and dangerous.

It was far better to try a **herb poultice** with cloth wrapping. One could sew up a wound with thread. And/or apply some honey.

Maggots were used on necrotized (dead) skin (*bleurgh*).

Broken bones would need to be pulled back into place, then a plaster made of comfrey paste or mud would be applied which would set into a hard cast. Another name for comfrey is knitbone.

Trepanning (or trephination) has been used since neolithic times. This is the procedure of drilling a hole into the patient's skull to relieve headaches, pressure or epilepsy. Most people actually survived!

And, before you scoff, it's still in use today. However, it's now part of neurosurgery – craniotomies – to remove epidural and subdural hematomas (brain bleeds). The removed piece of skull is normally replaced as quickly as possible, and kinder, modern surgical instruments are used.

Wine was seen as a restorative, so it wasn't all bad.

Along with physical treatments, prayer and penance were prescribed remedies, y'know, in case God was punishing the patient.

Other (detailed) Remedies
DO NOT TRY THESE AT HOME!!!

Some of these remedies may be **lethal**. Others may cause serious harm.

This information is for **FICTION USE ONLY!**

Have I made myself clear? Seriously, please **do not** try these out.

Vinegar was widely used in medicinal ways; from cleaning wounds to baths, mouthwash and drinks. Fine. However, here is a specific tonic:

Four Thieves Vinegar (plague prevention)
Take three pints of strong white wine vinegar, add a handful of each of wormwood, meadowsweet, wild marjoram and sage, fifty cloves, two ounces of campanula roots, two ounces of angelica, rosemary and horehound and three large measures of camphor. Place the mixture in a container for fifteen days, strain and express then bottle. Use by rubbing it on the hands, ears and temples from time to time when approaching a plague victim.

This also crops up under the name of Marseilles vinegar among others. Although medicated vinegars have been around since at least Hippocrates, this recipe is said to have originated during the Black Death by a band of, yes, four thieves who used it to prevent catching the plague whilst they raided houses of the deceased. Charming!?

It does seem to have worked, at least in part. And many of the ingredients are antimicrobial and flea repellent. BUT some ingredients are dangerous. NOT to be used today.

Almonds were said to aid sleep, provoke urination, and induce menstruation.

Apple Cider Vinegar (to reduce fever)

Mix one part apple cider vinegar with two parts of cold water. Soak a cloth and place it upon the forehead.

Cannabis

Originally sold in Egypt, it was eventually imported to England (and Europe). Became popular for its anxiety and pain-relieving properties.

Mint And Coriander (also for fever)

Whilst I'm looking at reducing fever, one could also boil water with leaves of mint and coriander. Drink 3-4 times a day.

Peppermint oil was ever so useful for all things gastrointestinal e.g. dysentery, dyspepsia, cramps and flatulence. But see the previous 'medicinal herbs' section for more information on mints.

Opium / Poppy (painkiller)

Opium, it is one of the world's oldest painkillers.

Opium poppies were well known long before the medieval era; since 3,400 BC when the Sumerians cultivated it in Mesopotamia and called it the "joy plant". It travelled to the Ancient Egyptians and Minoans. Traders took the opium flowers to Carthage, and Europe, where it spread to Persia, India and China. The "milky juice of the poppy" was mentioned in the 3rd century BC by Theophrastus. And the opium poppy was recognised in the 1st century AD by the likes of Pliny and Galen.

Later, in the 16th century, it was turned into laudanum. And even today, opiates can be found in the form of codeine etc. Great for pain relief, bad for addiction.

Anyway, in the 15th century, there was a mixture of hemlock, henbane and opium poppy – this is definitely one of the possibly fatal remedies. But it seems to have been used in small doses as a strong painkiller, and may even have been a rudimentary general anaesthetic.

Or grind the peel of the poppy stalk and mix with honey, to create a plaster for wounds.

Theriac (aka Venice Treacle)

An expensive, imported preparation which should be aged at least a year. It included up to 60 ingredients, including opium. Only to be used for adults, it was applied as an external salve. It became a 'cure-all'.

Bald's Leechbook

Yes, this Saxon book was a fine resource.

"Against hiccupy stomachs or swelling take horned cattle flesh cooked in vinegar and with oil thickened with salt and dill and leek, partake of that for a seven night, henceforth relieven thence the afflicted stomach." – in other words, some beef and oniony oil for a week for poorly tummies. I could go with that.

Of course, there were other remedies which were even less desirable. I'm still **not recommending** this. But as an example, to treat **gout**:

"Take an owl and pluck it clean and open it, clean and salt it. Put it in a new pot and cover it with a stone and put it in an oven and let it stand till it be burnt. And then stamp [pound] it with boar's grease and anoint the gout therewith."

btw **Gout** is an inflammatory form of arthritis. Uric acid deposits and tophi appear in and around the joints, causing pain and swelling. It's mainly caused by individuals consuming food that is high in purines — basically, all the meat, fish and alcohol of the rich in 15th century England contained purines. Hence gout being a common ailment then.

Another ailment caused by a rich diet was **constipation**. A remedy found in a monastic breviary (not the Leechbook) was to: *"take a pese of soepe, make hit smale and putt it yn youre fundamewnt and then rest upon your bed."* Yep, take a piece of soap and stick it up your…backside and lie down.

"In case that a man cannot retain his urine," burn the claws of a boar (or another swine) and sprinkle the ashes into his drink.

If someone had a nasty burn, create a salve of burnt goat excrement, wheat stalks, and butter. Heat over a fire and smear onto the skin.

Or one may create a whip of porpoise skin to use on lunatics – wtaf?!?

For back pain / sciatica: *"Take a spoonful of the gall of a red ox and two spoonfuls of water-pepper and four of the patient's urine, and as much cumin as half a French nut and as much suet as a small nut and break and bruise your cumin. Then boil these together till they be like gruel then let him lay his haunch bone (hip) against the fire as hot as he may bear it and anoint him with the same ointment for a quarter of an hour or half a quarter, and then clap on a hot cloth folded five or six times and at night lay a hot sheet folded many times to the spot and let him lie still two or three days and he shall not feel pain but be well."*

I think that's quite enough of those, don't you? Bleurgh! And I repeat, **DO NOT TRY THESE**. Please. I really don't want anything nasty to happen to you or your loved ones. Do not put that on my conscience. Please. Thank you.

Writing Prompt – Medicine

Uh, oh, is your MC feeling alright, babe?

- What disease have they caught?
- What cure can they obtain?
- Who are they going to call for?

Do tell them to be careful – even little cuts can get nasty infections in medieval England!

HYGIENE AND BEAUTY

I'd like to start by reminding you that cleanliness was actually important to medieval folk.

Bathing

The lord of the manor (or indeed, those in a monastery) may have their own bathing house at home. Whereas peasants may have to bathe in streams. Townspeople probably had access to a public bath house. Although, the latter were also places to partake of other naked activities (*nudge nudge, wink wink*).

Baths were basically barrels. One's faithful servant would fill it with heated water and herbs such as thyme - mmm...lovely. Although, this was quite arduous and would not be done very regularly in all likelihood. But pipes did carry the water away after, so there's that.

Some regarded immersing your whole body in water as detrimental to health. Whilst others simply couldn't afford the luxury. Even rich folk would wash in between baths. So, on a **daily basis**, with a rag/cloth/sponge and freshish water, they'd simply wash their important bits (underarms, nethers, hands and face).

Towels

What did they dry themselves with?

Well, you can use the word 'towel'. The Middle English word was "towayle" from the Old French "toaille". It's origins lie in words pertaining to cloth and to wash.

They were different from the towels we use today which are made typically of terry cloth; looped fabric. The towels of medieval England were linen cloths. From the 14th century, they even had pretty woven borders in indigo – fancy patterns could be used for the rich, or stripes.

These towels could be carried by servants waiting at tables. When large towels were laid across chairs reserved for the top guests at banquets, they were referred to as a 'surnappe'. Towels were also used in the birthing chamber.

Hair Washing

One's hair was secreted under a coif (linen cap) and/or other headwear (see 'Clothing/Fashion' for details).

Anyway, so nobody ever really saw hair. Even in bed, they would wear a head covering. A good combing should get rid of the worst debris. Combs were used, but hairbrushes don't seem to have been around.

So, hair didn't get washed much. And when it did, it was quite laborious, involving several rinses of different ingredients.

- ❖ The first rinse may have included lye from water heated with burned wine stems
- ❖ Then rinsed with plain hot water
- ❖ Oil/grease and lemon zest could be mixed and applied as a sort of conditioner
- ❖ And other scents may be added to perfume the hair

Soap

Soap was known and made in England by the 10th century.

One recipe calls for:

- Ashes from an oak tree
- Tallow – animal fat
- Lime – generally heated to become quicklime
- Salt
- Flour
- Water

Types of soap:

- **Castile soap** was white (from France). VERY expensive; for nobles only.
- **Grey soap** (from Bristol) – bit cheaper than Castile
- **Black soap** – in towns and cities, cheaper than white or grey but still expensive
- **Basic soap** for basic folk - Ash (which is alkali and means that in Arabic!). Water run through ash creates lye. Leftover/putrid animal fat (or olive oil if you could get it) would be mixed. Monks documented how stinky soapworks were, and that they had to be downwind of towns (alongside tanneries and slaughterhouses).

In an emergency, just a pinch of ash alone could help degrease hands. But this was dangerous as it may burn the skin (not from heat).

Herbs, such as sage were used to make a sort of **deodorant**.

Knights brought **perfume** back from The Crusades. Lavender and rose were popular ingredients.

Oral cleanliness - well, the first toothbrush was patented in 1857. However, that did not mean they didn't look after their mouths. Mouth rinses made of things such as vinegar and mint were used. They rubbed their teeth with a cloth. And just chewing some fresh herbs helped.

Shaving was obviously a thing. From the 15th century, steel-edged straight razors began to emerge. Whetstones were used to sharpen blades. And they seem to have used soap as shaving cream.

Toilets

I did mention toilets in our tour of the manor house rooms. However, I wanted to add a bit more.

So, yes, castles and manor houses had **garderobes** for the lord and lady (and chamber pots). But what about everybody else?

Peasants had a **'night soil bucket'**. Poo in one bucket, pee in a different pot. These would be disposed of in separate cesspits/midden heaps. Each had a different use.

But what if you're caught short in public? Well, there were **'common privies'** (public toilets) in the cities. Also known as 'common jakes', *'pissyngholes'* or 'house of easement'. There were thirteen of these in London, one of which apparently seated 84 people! All poo together!?

Public latrines were usually situated next to or near the main waterways, so pipes could carry the waste directly into those watercourses. Some were directly on bridges. Lovely!?

If visiting an **inn** or even a tavern, there were quite possibly barrels with planks over for one's use. These barrels would then be taken to the nearest cesspit to be emptied. But if staying overnight, there should also be a chamber pot.

Gong farmers would collect the waste from cesspits and moats (at night). They may be paid as much as 2s per tonne of waste.

The excrement was **useful** fertiliser. But the urine was used for washing clothes, quenching steel, dyeing wool and in the tanneries to remove hairs from leather.

Having said all this, there still seems to have been folk who poured their liquid waste from their windows into the street gulleys whilst crying out, "*Garde a l'eau!*" ('Watch out for the water').

Lube

Well, it's always been around in some form or another. And it's very important in certain situations. Please let your characters use it!

In the 15th century, one could use olive oil – it had been used in that way since the Ancient Greeks.

Clove oil could possibly be used, if you had access to it. Handy in that it has muscle relaxant and painkilling properties, apparently. And is still an ingredient in some modern lubes today.

Or, y'know, spit. Just saying. Really not advisable, but when desperate (*shrugs*).

Skincare and Beauty

I remember hearing how a pot of **moisturiser** had been found at an Ancient Roman site, and its contents were analysed. It contained similar ingredients to ones still in use today! So, it is perhaps not surprising to hear that cosmetics were in regular use from the 12th century all over Europe.

Ointments were mainly fat based, by the way. (*whispers*) They still are!

As with so many times in history, I'm sorry to say that smooth, pale skin was the desired look. If one was out of doors long enough to get a tan, one was probably a lowly labourer.

There were small, cosmetic **mirrors** from around the 13th century. Oh vanity, ever present!

Herbs and amethyst were used as complexion enhancers, especially if one had an outbreak of spots (*runs to crystal collection on my shelf to try*).

All sorts of concoctions were used; most of which were highly toxic. But hey, as my mother always told me, "You have to suffer to be beautiful!" (*PLEASE NOTE: I do NOT hold this to be true and use this here in sarcastic tones only).

Mind you, that rosewater brought back by the Crusaders is still prized for its skin healing properties as well as the delicious scent.

The good people also had little tools such as ear cleaners.

Oh, and I'll get more into fashion later, but using tweezers, ladies plucked their hairline for that gorgeous high forehead look (ever hear of someone being "highbrow"?). With the rest of their hair tucked under headwear, apparently, the bald look was in!? LOL

Even in the 14th century, **white lead powder** was being used to cover blemishes. This didn't stop until the late Georgians some 400 years later. Really? It took that long to realise it was making people ill, causing hair and tooth loss?

Hey, this technically goes further back. The Ancient Egyptians used black kohl for eyeliner - that too contained lead salts. Although, hopefully, in less harmful quantities. In fact, it's argued, that maybe it helped prevent eye infections and boosted the immune system.

But, I digress.

The Church, surprise, surprise, declared makeup to be the work of the devil! Did that stop them? Of course not.

In addition to the toxic white makeup, the rich mixed red roots with sheep fat to **redden their lips**. Failing that, rubbing a bit of lemon into one's lips naturally increased the blood flow; not technically makeup then, eh?

Want **blonde** hair? Sure, mix up some sheep's urine and saffron!

My heroine, Isabel, lived on a sheep farm. However, she was far too good to have done anything like the aforementioned sheep-assisted cosmetics. At least, none that I've admitted to in her story.

Seriously though, if you do find any medieval cosmetics recipes online, please don't try them at home - they probably won't end well. At best, serious skin reactions may occur. At worst, death!

Writing Prompt – Hygiene

What's that pong?

- So, what does your character smell like?
- Did they scrub their pits 'n bits today?
- Please tell me they washed their hands. What soap did they use?

FEMININE HYGIENE AND ALL THINGS CHILDBIRTH

WARNING: This section contains graphic descriptions. It also covers infertility and mortality.

Menstruation

OK, let's get straight into 'feminine hygiene' aka menstruation. It's natural and happens to around half the population. But what did they do about it back in the day?

All sorts of words were used for their periods, such as 'courses, menstra, termes or women's sickness'. But, whatever they called it, women have always had to cope with their menstrual cycles.

I mentioned earlier in 'medicine', how ladies used blood (sphagnum) moss to soak up their menstrual blood. This was quite probably stuffed into linen as a rudimentary sanitary towel. The moss was sometimes also used as toilet paper, by the way.

Due to lack of nutrition, however, periods may not have been monthly. They began around twelve years of age, and were an indication a young lady was ready to start producing children, and therefore could be wed. This is why it wasn't unheard of for girls aged fourteen to get married (*shudders*).

There were some odd beliefs around periods. Sadly, it was seen as a punishment from God, especially as nuns did not menstruate (allegedly). Again, I point out the lack of nutrition; nuns and very devout ladies would not have eaten much. But, y'know, let's not dwell.

Isabel in my book, *Love in the Roses*, challenges her husband to have his wicked way with her during her flow, but not to blame her if she then bore a deformed child. Yes, this was a belief held at that time! It was also why some children were born with red hair, obviously!?

Menstruating women may curdle the milk, so were kept away from activities such as cheese making.

And, as their excretions were 'so toxic', they were sometimes encouraged to roam around cornfields with their skirts pulled up, so they could act as an insect repellent. (Words fail me!)

But there was also help. Despite the common opinion that this bleeding/suffering was served to women from God and they should shut up and put up... there were herbal remedies to aid the pain. Lady's Mantle, parsley, thyme and woodruff were all used - because women help women.

Birth Control

It stands to reason that not every woman wished to become pregnant. Childbirth was incredibly dangerous; over one in three women died in their childbearing years! Plus, prostitutes have existed since the dawn of man, so they probably didn't want to become heavy with child either. And I hear tell some nuns were actually quite naughty - probably a good idea not to get pregnant in their case; the scandal and punishment - eek!

But, interfering with the will of God was, of course, sinful.

There was a papal bull against witchcraft which accused them of having, "slain infants yet in the womb" and "hindering men from performing the sexual act and women from conceiving". So, we know it happened. And as it was witches who were targeted, herbs were probably involved.

Again, I am not recommending trying any of these. And I cringe at the wording, but **herbs** such as pennyroyal, parsley and rue were considered an abortifacient. Wild carrot seed was believed to have contraceptive effects. Barrenwort (aka epimedium, bishop's hat or horny goat weed) was thought to cause sterility. There are even herbs today which still caution pregnant people not to use them. ~ These herbs would be brewed into concoctions.

As a **barrier**; the *Canon of Medicine Avicenna*, recommended inserting mint within the cervix before engaging in intercourse. Really not a good idea – don't stick things up there! However, back then, folk could also soak a cloth in vinegar or honey and poke it up. Even the Ancient Egyptians thought up a spermicide; "mix grated Acacia leaves and honey and soak a gauze to be inserted into the vagina." Seriously – in our modern world, there are better ways.

Infertility

On the flipside, there were women who definitely *did* want to become pregnant and maybe struggled to do so. Perhaps surprisingly, infertility was not always regarded as a woman's problem.

Naturally, one would be encouraged to pray. After all, you must have displeased God if he isn't allowing you to procreate. St Anne was patron saint for this. Or, one could make pilgrimage to St. Thomas Cantilupe's shrine in Hereford.

The physical weight of both parties was taken into consideration, according to the 12th century gynaecological text, *The Trotula*. If one was overweight, you could try sweating out the fat in a hot bath.

Of course, looking at urine was part of diagnosis too. Mix each person's wee with some wheat bran in a pot, and whoever's was smelliest and/or most ridden with worms after nine days was the one with the issue (eww!). If no worms were present, then the couple should be blessed with a child in God's own time.

Onions and parsnips were amongst foods encouraged for the man to help produce his seed.

Talking of seed, the medieval folk believed both men and women produced seed to produce offspring. So, **in order to conceive, the lady had to orgasm too** - hoorah!

I must say, I did cheer hearing that. Until I learned that this was then used *against* women as well – but of course it was (*eyeroll, smacks head*). If a woman was taken against her wishes and became pregnant it was therefore decided she must have enjoyed it so could not be considered rape (*angry screaming*).

Anyway, again, herbs and foods were recommended for altering the temperature of the woman's body so she could conceive.

To help protect against miscarriage, *The Trotula* suggests:

"Take oil, wax, powder of frankincence, and mastic, and mix them, and let the woman be annointed front and back two or three times a week. This very much strengthens the womb and the cotyledons."

If one wished to bring forth a man child, there was the recommendation from Dioscorides to make a drink of the stitchwort seed.

Pregnancy

But how did you know if you were pregnant?

Well, with irregular periods (usually among the poor), it could be quite tricky to tell. A woman may not know until she began to show or felt the "quickening" of the baby's first moves. And there was also the possibility of morning sickness.

However, wise women knew the secrets of urine — it is such an important bodily fluid! Simply pop a needle into your bowl of wee and see if it rusts.

The medical folk also looked at pee. Pale to white in colour with a cloudy surface indicated pregnancy.

Want to know if you're expecting a boy? Place a drop of milk from the mother's breast into water; if it sinks, it's a boy. If it floats, it's a girl.

Cravings

Galen again was referred to — such a helpful Ancient Greek. He noted that in the first three months of pregnancy, mothers may suffer from the incredibly bad humor, *citta*. This caused them to crave sour and bitter things, or even shells and extinguished coals.

To stem that, he recommended the occasional day of fasting (oh, sweet mercy!). Or many small meals preceded by water, followed by wine (can you imagine?). Food should be dry and astringent.

Walks, and fragrant but not too sweet white wine were also recommended.

Childbirth

Now, if you were poor, you'd work right up to the moment of labour, in all likelihood. So, let us look at the wealthy.

Ah, the 'lying in'. Before confining oneself to the bedchamber, a woman would attend church for a special blessing.

Only widows owned property, but some women were still permitted to make their last will & testament before the big event.

So, with all household and spiritual matters seen to, the expectant mother would retire to her chamber, four to six weeks before the baby was due. Only women allowed beyond this point!

The midwife, a woman, would enter the chamber. Mayhap, the good mother had female friends or relatives who would also be in attendance.

- ❖ The room was darkened; the curtains drawn
- ❖ Tapestries with relaxing scenes depicted were hung
- ❖ Fires were lit - the warmer the better
- ❖ Herbs were set asmoke and wafted around
- ❖ Crucifixes and religious icons would be strewn about

~ in short, the room was set to recreate the dark, warm, quiet womb.

The women would then spend time in quiet contemplation and doing everything they could to promote calm. The book of hours would be read frequently and muchly praying would be conducted.

Food would be controlled. Nothing too salty or containing rue or parsley. Small dishes of chicken, blackbird, mutton or partridge were advisable. Wine should be cut with water or balsam.

Daily hot baths were recommended. The hot water should be steeped with mallows, violets, linseed, fenugreek, chamomile and barley.

The mother's thighs and genitals would be anointed daily with oil of camomile, chicken fat, foam from the top of butter and *unguentum dialthaea* (an ointment made from marshmallow roots).

Walking was seen as beneficial exercise, perhaps up and down the stairs.

Argh, we reach **labour** itself!

Warm water which dates had been cooked in was seen as an energy-fortifying drink.

Again, with the oil and fat anointing! And/or apply a poultice.

Wearing coral around the neck was supposed to help ease pain. And she could clutch gemstones (such as jasper which would also help afterwards) or a magnet. Eaglestone may be tied to her thigh.

The woman would be encouraged to walk about as labour pains kicked in.

And time to pray extra hard!

In lieu of gas & air, the mother could clutch a holy relic or talisman. A **birthing girdle** may be placed upon her abdomen; a long, parchment (or hart's skin) scroll with saints such as The Virgin Mary, St Margaret or Julitta and Quiricus depicted.

The **birthing stool** was a popular aid in childbirth all the way through to around 1800. Funnily enough, men became midwives at that time too (*grumbly noises* - don't know what's best - *mumbles*).

Imagine a horseshoe-shaped stool. The woman could squat down upon this and let gravity come to her rescue. These stools could be treasured family heirlooms. Another woman could sit behind and cradle the poor mother. Isn't that nice?

The use of birthing stools shortens the birth canal and increases pelvic diameter. Doesn't that sound like a good idea? Hmm?

If the baby was round the wrong way, the midwife may oil her hands and, y'know, reach in.

Caesareans were a known thing. However, this was a last resort measure as it was highly likely neither mother nor baby would survive the procedure. Basically, the mother was either dead or dying before they'd try.

The midwife was permitted to baptize the baby, incidentally. But only if the baby was sickly - a quick blessing before it died was necessary so its soul could still reach heaven. (This is all terribly morbid; I do apologise.)

However, once the baby was out (hopefully without intervention), then the **umbilical cord** needed to be dealt with. It could be cut, and powdered dragon's blood (plant resin) sprinkled on. Or tie it off with twisted wool. After it dropped off, the umbilical cord was often thrown onto the fire in the room - this was a way of purifying the sinful origins of conception!

Herbs were lit and wafted under the mother's nose. This would cause her to sneeze, but her nose would be pinched. Therefore, the pressure would be sent downwards so she could expel the afterbirth.

More from *The Trotula*: "*For pain of the vagina after birth, take rue, mugwort, and camphor, grind them well and, having prepared them with musk oil or pennyroyal oil and warmed them in a pot, wrap them in a cloth and insert as a suppository.*"

A needle and thread could have come in handy too. (Oh, this is all making me wince without any anaesthetic!) But there is more medical advice: "*For rupture of the lower parts after birth, take root of comfrey, dry it and then pulverise it well, and put with fine powder of cumin and also cinnamon in the vagina, and it will be solidified.*"

And if that sneeze didn't expel the afterbirth...

"*For birth of the womb and for bringing out the afterbirth. Take root of parsley, leaves of leek, and borage, and extract the juice, and mix in a little oil, and give to the patient to drink, and put vinegar into the vagina, and she will be freed.*"

Pennyroyal was also a good herb for such expulsions.

That coral amulet hung about the mother's neck during childbirth - a similar one could now be placed upon the infant for protection. Either that or amber.

Mother and baby would be bathed. Injuries seen to. The baby encouraged to urinate by squeezing on its bladder.

Then the baby needed to be **swaddled**. Their bones were seen as weak and not fully formed, so swaddling helped keep them in shape until they grew stronger. This would be done at least until the child could sit up on its own or it reached the age of one year.

The mother may have been given some **caudle**. This is a dish of egg yolks, ale/wine, sugar and saffron (recipes vary). A basic dish accessible to all and seen as a restorative.

And hopefully, both were healthy and would be able to have a bit of a sleep. I think they'd earned it!

But this was not the end. Oh no. Mother and baby would be kept in confinement for another four to six weeks, whilst both gained their strength and healed.

Breast Feeding

The mother could put a bit of honey on her breast to encourage the baby to suckle (*aww*). Baby should be fed three times per day. And the mother would learn when to unswaddle so her child could relieve itself. She'd then wrap it back up, snug as a bug in a rug.

Wet nurses could be used, but it was deemed best for the mother to perform this duty if she could. The Church deemed that if it was good enough for The Virgin Mary, any mother should do so.

Breast feeding was encouraged until around the age of two.

Gnawing on roots of liquorice or gladioli could help when **teething** pains kicked in. Umm...gladioli are highly toxic!

Fun fact: Breast feeding was thought to delay menses and prevent pregnancy (for six months); free contraception. And it does indeed help lessen the likelihood of conceiving.

Baptism was essential for newborns. It could not wait until the mother was out of her confinement. So, the father (or appointed other if he were not present) would take the baby to church, along with the nominated godparents.

At the church door, prayers would be issued, whilst the priest made the sign of the cross three times.

The godparents would then recite the Lord's Prayer, Hail Mary and Creed, in Latin, of course.

Then, the baby was taken inside to the font. Holy oil was added to the water therein, and more prayers were recited. The godparents renounced Satan and pledged their faith.

The baby was anointed with holy oil and then baptised with three immersions in the name of the Father, Son and Holy Ghost.

The baby's forehead was then anointed with sacred chrism (holy oil) and a white chrisom cloth was bound round it as a symbol of the cleansing of its sins, and was kept in place for the following week.

Finally, the child was dressed in a white chrisom robe, which, if the child died within a month, was used as a shroud. I do apologise for such grim detail, but infant mortality rate was high, and one must bear this in mind.

The child was given a blessed candle, which therefore had the power when lit, to banish the Devil.

Churching

This chrisom cloth was then given to the mother for her Churching.

Yes, at the end of her confinement, the mum would go to church for her blessing. Please note, this was a ceremony for the mother, not the father. The woman had to be cleansed of the sin of conception. The father was not deemed "unclean" and attended the baptism as happy as Larry. Last time I checked, it takes two to tango, but there we are. It's what they did.

Anyway, the mother was met at the church door by the priest who carried holy water and candles.

The mother would have worn a veil and may have held a burning candle. She would issue forth said chrisom cloth and any other offerings.

The priest said a prayer of thanksgiving and asked for eternal life for the mother. Two Psalms were then read. And then the mother may have been sprinkled with holy water before being led into the church with a prayer of access.

A special Mass would then be conducted, with the mother offering thanks for the safe delivery of her child. She would also receive Communion.

She was then able to resume daily activities, cleansed of all that sin.

At the end of all that, one presumably continued to pray that your child continued strong and healthy.

Around 30% of children died before the age of five. Yikes!

At the age of seven, presumably when parents relaxed a little bit, boys may be sent off for training, either ecclesiastical/scholar or as a knight. Girls may well have been sent to another household to learn the ways of management of such.

And then they'd be married off. And the cycle began anew!

Writing Prompt – Women's Things

Eurgh, it's that time of month and there's no ibuprofen in sight. Not even a hot water bottle.

- Is your MC (or any of their friends) female?
- Are their 'courses' going to interfere with proceedings?
- Will they get pregnant?
- And what can they expect in the birthing chamber?

RELIGION

I spoke generally of religion before. But let us look more into the 15th century Church.

The Dissolution aka The Reformation didn't happen until 1536-1540. Before that, Cardinal Wolsey had started his investigations in 1519.

Even Martin Luther hadn't posted his infamous "Ninety-Five Theses", condemning the excesses and corruption in the Catholic Church, on the church door in Wittenburg, Germany until 1517. For context; this is viewed as the catalyst for the Protestant movement.

i.e. All that happened in the 16th century.

So, we had the Catholic church in England. Albeit with quiet rumbles of dissent in the background.

The Hierarchy of the Catholic Church

- ✟ The Pope
- ✟ Cardinals
- ✟ Archbishops
- ✟ Bishops
- ✟ (Parish) Priests / Abbots (of abbeys)
- ✟ Arch Deacons / Priors (in priories)
- ✟ Deans / Sub-Priors
- ✟ Monks

The Archbishop of Canterbury was the 'primate of All England' – the prelate of the Catholic Church in England (and apparently nothing at all to do with monkeys). And pretty much the only **cardinal** in the country. The cardinals were (and still are) the chaps who wore a red hat and were the only ones who could elect (or become) Pope.

Archbishops – Oversaw several dioceses (an area containing more than one congregation).

Bishops were ordained priests, responsible for a diocese. They ruled the priests and monasteries in their jurisdiction and received the taxes from such. Like priests, they conducted weddings, performed last rites, settled disputes, heard/absolved confession.

Chaplains were part of the household (for noble families). They would conduct daily Mass and recite prayers for the family (living and dead). They generally came from more humble origins. Think of him as a private priest.

Rectors and parish priests were involved in pastoral care for the community and earned a good living. Priests conducted Mass for the community and offered spiritual guidance. It's worth noting that priests were exempt from paying tax due to their noble profession.

Nuns and monks remained mostly in their cloisters and monasteries where they would help look after the sick, provide travellers with a place to stay and sometimes looked after people's financial matters.

NB Monasteries would often house libraries of diverse works.

Friars lived and worked in the community (not in a monastery) and were mendicant (reliant on alms).

They would travel in pairs and spread gossip at the dinner tables they were welcomed to. Although, a lot of men didn't look kindly upon friars as they thought they were taking money from the poor they were supposed to protect.

A **visiting clergyman** could have several purposes for their visit; charitable, spiritual, social, commercial or administrative.

This hierarchy then ties in with the buildings:
- **Cathedral** – run by a bishop
- **Abbey** – run by an abbot or abbess
- **Priory** – run by a prior or prioress

Abbeys and priories were types of **monastery** (or convents for the nuns); a self-contained religious community.

Types of Religious Communities

- ✟ **Monks (& Nuns)** – spent their life in a monastery (or convent), received sacred orders, took the Vow of Stability to their specific monastic community
- ✟ **Friars** – lived out in the world, were mendicant; were reliant on others for their survival, came from Franciscan or Dominican orders – wore brown robes
- ✟ **Canons** – priests living in a community, pledged a Vow of Stability to their abbey church or profession

All of these people sought to live a life of poverty, chastity and prayer.

I could probably write a whole book on monks and monasteries. However, I shan't bore you with details. But it is important to know they didn't all wear brown, as is perhaps the image you have of monks. Nor could just anyone become one.

Generally, one's parents donated a large sum of money or preferably a good parcel of land when offering up offspring to join a monastic order. This is partly how the Church came to own so much land in England. The postulant (the one applying to go in) was probably the second or third child, and quite possibly had been educated in a monastic school in preparation. They would enter the monastery at around sixteen years old (or any age after that).

NB Oblates (young children donated to monasteries) ceased to be a practice in the 12th century.

Folk with not much to offer could become lay brothers (or sisters) – effectively labourers in the monastery who were religious but didn't take vows.

The main orders of monks in England were:

- **Benedictines** – founded in 6th century by St Benedict, wore all **black** hence the nickname The Black Monks, most common order in England (several hundred houses), committed to writing, day centred around communal prayer, "pray and work" motto.

- **Cluniacs** – founded in 909, all its monasteries were daughters to the one in Cluny (France) and therefore priories, believed Benedictines had become too lax and involved too greatly in secular affairs, their main focus was on art, architecture and elaborate services, not really popular in England; only had around 50 houses. Most of their time was spent in prayer whilst wearing fine, **black** linen robes and silk vestments, whilst they employed workers to do their physical labour.

- **Augustinians** – founded 1061 by St Augustine, "The Black Canons" or "Austin Friars", wore **black robes with a white rochet** and a cap instead of a hood, priests (not monks), around 200 houses plus 356 hospitals incl. St Bartholemew, forbidden to look upon women, charity was their main focus.

- **Carthusians** – founded 1084, "The Silent Monks", "The White Monks", or "The Charter House Monks", the most austere of all the orders, lived in solitary cells, purely vegetarian, only about 9 houses in England. Wore undyed/**white**/ivory coloured tunics and cowls.

- **Cistercians** – founded in 1098, also called "The White Monks", most valued manual labour, believed Cluniacs were too opulent, followed a more literal adoption of The Rule, usually more plain and rural monasteries. They wore white tunics with either a black or white scapula (varies).

Everyday Folk Worship

That's probably quite enough about monks. What did religion look like to the laity (the everyday folk)? Well, everyone was expected to go to church for Mass every Sunday. But with the services being held in Latin, not everyone would have understood what they were listening to. But there was also confession to be made.

Songs were more Gregorian chants sung by a choir (not hymns sung by the congregation).

The church was a social hub as well, and events were held there on top of the usual baptisms, weddings and funerals.

The nave and tower belonged to people of the parish. They would pay a tithe (tax) of a tenth of their income to Church, which was spent on the parish priest, bishop, maintenance and the poor.

Manor courts were often held in the nave. And in the churchyard, they'd hold parties, plays, pageants and games (including football). Fortunately, monks brewed ale, so this would be part of the festivals.

But it was also a place of education. About one in ten peasants could become low level clergy.

Marriage

What age did people get married? Well, when data was collected from many records, it seems that the average age for a woman to marry in 15th century England was actually 27. However, that is an average.

Depending on their monetary worth, **girls were often married off in their teens, and the boys in their early twenties**. Royalty could marry off their princesses at age 12, but with the expectation that it wasn't consummated until age 14.

Weirdly, peasants were often freer to choose their marriage partner.

The UK marriageable age wasn't really legally dictated until the **Marriage Act of 1753**, which merely stated that a person under the age of 21 must have the consent of parents or guardians. It also stipulated that ceremonies must be conducted in a parish church or chapel of the Church of England and that banns must've been called or a licence obtained.

Generally, marriages were of the arranged variety. The fathers would have contracts drawn up, with details of the girl's dowry.

And a notice would be put up on the church door - the banns.

Age of Consent

In terms of Secular Law (as opposed to the Canon Law of the Church), in 1275, the Statute of Westminster made it a misdemeanour to "ravish a maiden within age." – this was interpreted to mean the age of marriage. Ergo, the first age of consent for girls in England was set at **12 years old**.

It was raised to 13 years old in 1875 and then taken up to 16 in 1885, where it has remained ever since in Great Britain. If you're writing about Ireland, you may want to check further as they had slightly different laws.

Incidentally, there is historical evidence to show that people have always had sex outside of marriage. Whilst at others, particularly amongst the poor, it was secretly encouraged so the family knew the girl could get pregnant!

But let is focus on the actual marriage part...

The Wedding Ceremony

Regardless of class, the wedding party would wear their finest clothes. Blue or green were popular colours for the bride. But both the bride and the groom may have worn a blue ribbon garter below their knee.

If the happy couple were of noble birth, there may be a procession including minstrels.

The groom could have a best man who would wear his sword, for he was the best swordsman and was there for protection. He would ride his horse behind the couple.

The bride would stand on the groom's left **at the church door**. And the priest would check they were of marriageable age, not related, the father gave his consent as well as the bride and groom.

The dowry agreement would then be read aloud.

The groom may then offer the bride a purse of coins which she'd distribute to the eagerly awaiting poor after the ceremony.

The **vows** would then be proclaimed. First by means of the groom declaring, ""I pledge to you that I will take you to be my wife and spouse within forty days, if holy Church agrees."

With the bride replying, ""I pledge to you that I will take you to be my husband and master within forty days, if holy Church agrees."

The priest would then recite a short homily on the sanctity of marriage.

The groom, holding his bride's hand would then announce, "I, (name), take thee, (name), to my wedded wife, to have and to hold from this day forward, for better, for worse, for richer, for poorer, for fairer or fouler, in sickness and in health, to love and to cherish, till death us depart, if holy church will ordain, and thereto I plight thee my troth."

The bride would declare, ""I, (name), take thee (name), to my wedded husband, to have and to hold from this day forward, for better for worse, for richer or poorer, in sickness and in health, to be bonny and buxom at bed and at board, to love and to cherish, till death us depart, according to God's holy ordinance; and thereto I plight thee my troth."

The priest would then bless the wedding ring (given to the bride only) and the special coins.

The groom would take the ring and first place it upon the bride's left index finger. "With this ring I thee wed."

Removing then placing the ring on her third finger, he followed with, "With my body I thee honour."

Finally, it was moved to her fourth finger. "And I endow you with the dowry agreed upon by my friends and yours."

The priest would then join their right hands together and announce, "Those whom God hath joined together let no man put asunder. Forasmuch as (name) and (name) have consented together in holy wedlock, and have witnessed the same before God and this company, and thereto have given and pledged their troth each to the other, and have declared the same by giving and receiving of a ring, and by joining of hands; I pronounce therefore that they be Man and Wife together, in the Name of the Father, and of the Son, and of the Holy Spirit. Amen."

The coins could then be distributed, and the wedding party would **enter the church** for a special Mass, with a canopy held over them by their assistants as they knelt at the altar. At its conclusion, the priest would offer a kiss of peace to the groom who would pass it on to the bride. And a final blessing was given.

A handy baby may then have been placed in the bride's arms outside the church as a blessing of fertility.

Then it was off home for a big feast.

Afterlife

One wished to minimise time spent in purgatory - the place where souls were purged of their sins before entering heaven (presuming they weren't sent to Hell). This is why people went on pilgrimage, for instance.

The local gentry would bestow patronage to the local church, and would be responsible for the chantry (and altar). This is where dedicated priests and singing clerks would chant/pray for their departed souls.

Performing good deeds and acts of charity were perceived as the best way to earn your place in heaven. This could include giving alms, but also giving paupers left-over food. And of course, donations of money/food/building maintenance to Church didn't go amiss.

One would observe the one year anniversary of the passing of a loved one out of respect but also, y'know, reducing purgatory time.

So, there was a **list of good deeds** created – to avoid purgatory but also because it encourages folk to live a life of love and compassion.

The Seven Corporal Acts of Mercy

1. Feed the poor
2. Give drink to the thirsty
3. House the stranger
4. Clothe the naked
5. Visit the sick
6. Relieve the prisoner
7. Bury the dead (like that's optional!?)

On the flipside, there is a **list of vices** which are likely to encourage further immorality. They were first enumerated by Pope Gregory I (the Great) in the 6th century and elaborated in the 13th century by St. Thomas Aquinas.

The Seven Deadly Sins

1. Vainglory, or pride
2. Greed, or covetousness
3. Lust, or inordinate or illicit sexual desire
4. Envy
5. Gluttony, which is usually understood to include drunkenness
6. Wrath, or anger
7. Sloth

However, these could be overcome by the:

Seven Heavenly Virtues

1. Humility
2. Charity
3. Chastity
4. Gratitude
5. Temperance
6. Patience
7. Diligence

Purgatory

Just in case you're confused, purgatory is "the state of those who die in God's friendship, assured of their eternal salvation, but who still have need of purification to enter into the happiness of heaven." It's not hell or perdition. It's more of a making up for mild wrong-doing; an in-between place for the not-quite-pure but not truly bad folk.

At the Second Council of Lyon in 1274, the Catholic Church defined its teaching on purgatory:

- ❖ some saved souls need to be purified after death
- ❖ such souls benefit from the prayers and pious duties that the living do for them

Different Levels of Sin

Mortal sin

"Mortal sin is sin whose object is grave matter and which is also committed with full knowledge and deliberate consent."

St Augustine defined it as, "something said, done, or desired contrary to the eternal law, or a thought, word, or deed contrary to the eternal law as a voluntary act."

A gravely sinful act can lead to damnation if a person does not repent of the sin before death. A sin is considered to be "mortal" when its quality is such that it leads to a separation of that person from God's saving grace.

Grave Matter

A criterion for mortal sin. It is specified in the Ten Commandments, "Do not murder, do not commit adultery, do not steal, do not bear false witness, do not defraud, honour your father and your mother."

By the way, if it's involuntary, it's a material sin.

Venial (lesser) Sin

Venial means forgivable. It consists of acting as one should not, but does not break one's friendship with God, only injures it.

It "weakens charity, manifests a disordered affection for created goods, and impedes the soul's progress in the exercise of the virtues and the practice of the moral good; it merits temporal punishment", for "every sin, even venial, entails an unhealthy attachment to creatures, which must be purified either here on earth, or after death in the state called Purgatory.

One does not have to confess a venial sin, but must complete penance for it.

What kind of sin was committed can be assessed by asking the following three questions:

1. Did the act involve a grave matter?
2. Was the act committed with full knowledge of the wrongdoing that had been done in the act?
3. Was the act done with full consent of the will?

Perdition

A *state* of eternal punishment; damnation, hell, absolute ruin.

Hell

A *place* where evil resides and where people may be confined to after death - a punishment for their behaviour during their life.

Penance

A voluntary self-punishment to show repentance (sorrow) for one's sin.

One would confess sins to a priest, receive a blessing and an instruction on how best to atone. This could be in the form of:

- ✞ Fasting
- ✞ Giving alms / church fines
- ✞ Reciting psalms
- ✞ Practicing celibacy
- ✞ Prayers

To count the prayers uttered, even in the 15th century (and long before), there were rosary/paternoster beads. Both the Our Father and the Hail Mary were recited. Reciting 150 paternosters was the equivalent to reciting the 150 Psalms.

- ✞ The Lord's Prayer on the large bead
- ✞ The Hail Mary on each of the ten adjacent small beads
- ✞ The Glory Be on the space before the next large bead
- ✞ The Hail Holy Queen (sometimes with other prayers, while holding the medal or large bead)
- ✞ The Sign of the cross.

There was a large body of work written by Burchard, the Bishop of Worms - *Burchard's Decretum of 1003*. He wrote out huge lists of sins and penances across twenty books (other penitentials were available).

Examples of penance:

- Breaking into a cemetery, digging out someone's grave and taking their clothes - two years penance with fasting.
- Refusing to attend prayers or mass or making offerings to married priests - one year's penance with appointed fast days.
- **Nightly emissions**: A person who willingly pollutes himself during sleep should wake up and chant nine psalms in a specified order. At the end of each psalm, he should kneel! For the following day, he shall eat nothing but bread and water. If he doesn't want to repay by sacrificing his food, then the alternative is to chant thirty psalms and kneel after completing each of them.

However, if the person who sins during sleep and has polluted himself *unintentionally* should chant 15 psalms. The man who sins but is not polluted will have to chant 24 psalms.

Men with men:

- He who **often** commits fornication with a man or with a beast should do penance for ten years.
- He who **after his twentieth year** defiles himself with a male shall do penance for fifteen years.
- Interfemoral sex (rubbing the penis between the thighs) - one year's penance.

NB Burchard of Worms specified sex with a married man, but did not give penance for unmarried ones specifically!

Women with women:

- ✠ If a woman practices vice with a woman, she shall do penance for three years.
- ✠ If she practices solitary vice, she shall do penance for the same period.
- ✠ The penance of a widow and of a girl is the same. She who has a husband deserves a greater penalty if she commits fornication.

Oral sex:

- ✠ He who ejaculates into the mouth of another shall do penance for seven years; **this is the worst of evils.** Elsewhere it was his judgment that both (participants in the offence) shall do penance to the end of life; or twelve years, or as above seven.

There you have it – oral sex was the worst sin! But do remember, **the very fact that these were listed means people were doing them**! This was the Church trying to regulate the populace. It does not mean the rules were obeyed.

Obviously, my research tended to drift into sex-related penance. I found it interesting to reflect that although same-sex fornication was clearly frowned upon, it was a venial/lesser sin. And one which could be pardoned with penance.

NB *All of these* were 'venial/lesser' sins which could be overcome with penance.

Feast Days

For most people, the main feast days included:

- ✟ **06 January** - Epiphany
- ✟ **02 Feb** – Candlemas (day dedicated to The Purification of the Virgin Mary)
- ✟ **(some time between 22 March and 25 April)** – Easter Sunday
- ✟ **25 Mar** – Annunciation of the Blessed Virgin Mary
- ✟ **(late May/early June)** - Corpus Christi - The Thursday after Trinity Sunday (60 days after Easter)
- ✟ **24 June** – Festival of St. John the Baptist
- ✟ **01 Aug** – Lammas (harvest festival)
- ✟ **10 / 11 Oct** – Michaelmas (on Julian calendar. 29 Sep on Gregorian)
- ✟ **01 Nov** – All Saints (aka All Hallows Day / Hallowmas)
- ✟ **11 Nov** – Martinmas (start of agricultural winter)
- ✟ **25 Dec** – Christmas Day
- ✟ **26 Dec** – St Stephen
- ✟ **28 Dec** – Childermas / Holy Innocents

The congregation would attend Mass on these days and have some sort of feast or celebration afterwards. This was kind of the bare minimum.

Fast Days

Lent is one of the most widely known periods of fasting. Shrove Tuesday, now better known as Pancake Day, used the last of the perishable goods. The next day, Ash Wednesday, started the 40 days straight of fasting — basically, a lot of fish was eaten.

- **Ash Wednesday and Good Friday were "black fasts."** These consisted of taking only one meal per day of bread, water and herbs after sunset. Thus marking the start and end of Lent.
- Other days of Lent - no food until 3pm (the hour of Our Lord's death). But water (and watered-down beer or wine) was allowed.
- No animal meats or fats
- No eggs
- No dairy products

There were also **Ember Days** — a three-day period of prayer and fasting which recurs four times over the course of the year. They occur on the **Wednesday, Friday and Saturday** of the weeks following:

- The first Sunday in Lent
- Whitsun
- The Feast of the Exaltation of the Cross (14 September)
- St Lucy's Day (13 December)

Why on those specific three days?

- ♱ Wednesday is in memory of Judas' betrayal
- ♱ Friday is in memory of the crucifixion
- ♱ Saturday is in memory of the tomb

There were also **Rogation Days** during Eastertide. These were more an abstinence from meat as opposed to actual fasting. There was the Major Rogation on 25th April, and the Minor Rogation Days on the Monday, Tuesday and Wednesday before the Ascension. The Greater and Lesser Litanies are prayed on those days respectively, and the crops are blessed. And there would have been religious processions too.

No wonder they celebrated Easter Sunday so well. That feast must have been utter blessed relief!

Oh, and then there were the fast days of Advent too — every Wednesday, Friday and Saturday after Martinmas until Christmas Day (another 40 day period).

So, religiously observant folk in the 15th century could be fasting for around a third of the year.

May Day

This is NOT a religious day, but I probably won't get the chance to mention it elsewhere. In fact, the church often condemned the celebration. But it was a popular one, nonetheless.

It falls on the 1st May and is a celebration of spring. Its origins seem rooted in the Roman, *Floralia* — a fertility celebration. The Pagan festival of Beltane also shares links with it.

Maids (young women) would go out first thing in the morning and wipe the dew over their hands and face for good luck and healing. One wished to reduce blemishes before trying to attract a man! Older women were known to do the same, in fairness.

The May Pole was a large tree trunk, erected in the centre of the village. People would decorate it with tree boughs, and indeed tie ribbons around it. In reality, it's a giant phallic symbol, but hey, moving on.

Love and fertility were the main focus. Flowers would decorate everywhere, songs were sung, games were played, and a good time was had. There was often a bonfire as part of the celebrations.

It's actually still celebrated in parts of Britain now. Tremendous fun!

Fun fact: bonfire is a contraction of bone fire, and actual animal bones used to be included in such.

Other such important days were:

Monday Plough / Plough Monday on 6th January — the day that agricultural work began; fields would be blessed. And a ploughshare was taken into church the day before for a special service of prayers, then paraded through the village along with musicians and dancers to raise money.

Hocktide – the Monday and Tuesday two weeks after Easter.

On Hock (or Hoke) Monday, the young women of the parish would grab the men off the street and tie them up. Upon receiving a release fee, they'd be let go. The ransom was then donated to the parish church fund.

On Hock Tuesday, the men got to return the 'favour'.

Sheep Shearing Day – in mid-June, before St John the Baptist day (24th June). In areas where sheep farming was practiced, they held this event each year. Well, the wool trade was incredibly important to the economics of the land. After shearing the sheep, a great feast would be held within the community.

Saints

Other Saint's Days would be celebrated on a regional or even household basis. The manor house inhabitants may have preferred saints they paid their respects to, even representing them in stained glass windows or the rood screens they paid for in the church.

Many would flock to the manor house for a good nosh and knees up (medieval style) to celebrate (by invitation).

Females were also celebrated. Obviously, the Blessed Virgin Mary had her own celebrations and was often depicted. But so was Mary Magdalene.

There were also female saints, such as the three virgin martyrs: Aplollonia, Barbara and Dorothy. They were popularised in entertaining stories as defiant saints, defending chastity. I'm mentioning them here as they don't seem to appear in liturgical lists normally.

- ✠ **St Apollonia** (feast day 09 Feb) - protected her devotees from toothache.
- ✠ **St Barbara** (04 Dec) - was/is the patroness of miners, fire-work makers, artillerymen, stone-makers & fortifications. She protects against sudden death, lightning, subsiding mines, cannon-balls & impenitence. Basically, a warfare saint (and now engineers!). And probably the original Rapunzel!
- ✠ **St Dorothy** - was venerated on 06 Feb, when trees are blessed. She is the patron saint of gardeners, brewers, brides, florists, midwives and newlyweds.
- ✠ On 18 Aug, **St Helena** was celebrated - Mother of Constantine The Great, she was an inspirational figurehead to women.

Incidentally, from the late 15th / early 16th Century, St George's dragon was portrayed as female! Just as Protestantism was taking over. Women were being made more obedient at this time. Worth noting.

You know what? I wasn't going to list all the saints' days because I was worried this is all getting a bit listy. However, it's useful to have a point of reference for all the potential days of celebration, so I will.

Not many folk would have observed all these days. My monks in *Love Habit* clearly did, though. For purely devout reasons and nothing at all to do with the excuse to eat meat, of course.

Anyway, this is as best as I can make out, all the days of celebration for the Catholic Church in 15th century England. They were using the Julian calendar. Plus, some of these dates later got changed, so don't get troubled. And some, like Easter, are just downright confusing!

By the way, I did find a really helpful calculator online to find out when Easter was in any given year, on 'medieval genealogy', but the link says it's not secure, so I won't include it here. And I draw the line at typing out 100 lines of Easter Sunday dates in this book. Just know such references exist should you need to find out.

The Liturgical Year

I'll start with January for ease of reference.

- ✟ **01 Jan** - Octave of Christmas / The Feast of the Circumcision of Jesus
- ✟ **05 Jan** - Twelfth Night (Theophany, or Three Kings Day); eve of Epiphany – end of Christmastide
- ✟ **06 -13 Jan** - The Octave of Epiphany (8 days)
- ✟ **20 Jan** - Sts Fabian and Sebastian
- ✟ **21 Jan** - St Agnes
- ✟ **22 Jan** - St Vincent
- ✟ **02 Feb** - Candlemas / Candelaria Festival / Purification of the Virgin Mary
- ✟ **05 Feb** - St Agatha
- ✟ **14 Feb** - St Valentine
- ✟ **25 Feb** - St Matthias
- ✟ March/April - Easter Sunday could occur any time between 22 March and 25 April
- ✟ **Shrove Tuesday** - 6 ½ weeks before Easter Sunday - Ash Wednesday began Lent ("black fast")
  Ember Days (hard fast & prayer; Wed, Fri & Sat following Ash Wednesday)
- ✟ **Sunday before Easter** - Palm Sunday was the last week of Lent; start of Holy Week which then incl. Maundy Thursday, Good Friday ("black fast")
- ✟ **Easter Sunday**
- ✟ **12 Mar** - St Gregory
- ✟ **21 Mar** - St Benedict
- ✟ **25 Mar** - Annunciation (aka Lady Day) - 9 months before Christmas; Gabriel visited Mary (and the **new calendar year began**)
  (if 25th Mar falls either in Holy Week or in Easter Week, the feast is postponed to the Mond after the Second Sunday of Easter)
- ✟ **23 Apr** - St George
- ✟ *Mon, Tues & Wed before Ascension - Rogationtide (3 day fast)*
- ✟ 40 days after Easter -   Ascension Thursday
- ✟ 7 days after Rogation - Pentecost / Whitsunday (Whitsun Week)

- ☦ *Ember Days (Wed, Fri & Sat following Whitsun)*
- ☦ **Trinity Sunday** (first Sun after Pentecost) - end of Whitsun Week
- ☦ **11 May** - Sts Phillip and James
- ☦ **Corpus Christi** (second Thurs after Pentecost) – *pageants and plays held*
- ☦ **11 Jun** - St Barnabas
- ☦ **24 Jun** - Festival of St John the Baptist
  (Pagan Summer Solstice day before) – bonfires and processions
- ☦ **29 Jun** - Sts Peter and Paul
- ☦ **02 Jul** - The Visitation of the Virgin to her cousin Elizabeth
- ☦ **20 Jul** - St Margaret of Antioch
- ☦ **22 Jul** - St Mary Magdalene
- ☦ **25 Jul** - St James
- ☦ **26 Jul** - The Feast of Saint Anne, mother of the Virgin
- ☦ **01 Aug** - LAMMAS and harvest festival AND The Feast of St. Peter at the Chains - *morality & mystery plays*
- ☦ **06 Aug** - The Transfiguration of Jesus
- ☦ **10 Aug** - St Lawrence
- ☦ **15 Aug** - Assumption of the Virgin Mary
- ☦ **24 Aug** - St Bartholomew
- ☦ **29 Aug** - Beheading of St John the Baptist
- ☦ **08 Sep** - Nativity of the Virgin Mary
- ☦ **14 Sep** - The Exaltation of the Holy Cross
  Ember Days (Wed, Fri & Sat following The Exaltation)
- ☦ **21 Sep** - St Matthew
- ☦ **29 Sep** - Michaelmas
- ☦ **09 Oct** - St Denis
- ☦ **28 Oct** - Sts Simon and Jude
- ☦ **01 Nov** - All Saints
- ☦ **02 Nov** - All Souls
- ☦ **11 Nov** - Martinmas *(feast of goose or beef)*
  Following day, Advent fasting began; every Mon/Wed/Fri until Christmas Day
- ☦ **22 Nov** - St Cecilia
- ☦ **23 Nov** - St Clement
- ☦ **25 Nov** - St Katharine
- ☦ **30 Nov** - St Andrew

- ✞ **06 Dec** - St Nicholas (*appointment of 'Boy Bishop'*)
- ✞ **13 Dec** - St Lucys Day
  (*also Pagan Winter Solstice; shortest day*)
- ✞ *Ember Days (Wed, Fri & Sat following St Lucy's Day)*
- ✞ **21 Dec** - St Thomas the Apostle
- ✞ **25 Dec** - Christmas Day
  (*Solemnity of the Nativity the Lord, the Birth of Jesus Christ, and the First Day in the Octave of Christmas*)
- ✞ **26 Dec** - St Stephen
- ✞ **27 Dec** - St John the Evangelist
- ✞ **28 Dec** - The Feast of the Holy Innocents / Childermas
- ✞ **29 Dec** - St Thomas Becket
- ✞ **31 Dec** - St Silvester

I know this is a long list, but hopefully it will give you some dates to think about – either quiet contemplation or big celebration.

And, just to reiterate; some of these dates are different from those celebrated by the Catholic Church today.

Pilgrimage

Thanks to Geoffrey Chaucer's *Canterbury Tales*, most people have at least heard of the pilgrimage to the shrine of St Thomas Becket in Canterbury. His book covers the period 1387-1400 and was written in Middle English — quite hard to read but is full of medieval life (even sex!).

Fun fact: the demise of Thomas Becket earned King Henry II an actual whipping!

Other shrines one could visit to seek penance, absolution from sin or relief from illness were those of: Edward the Confessor in Westminster Abbey, Richard of Chichester, Thomas Cantilupe of Hereford, St Osmund of Salisbury or John of Bridlington.

(*coughs*) Many shrines were built on old pagan sites – just saying.

As I make mention of the shrine of St. Thomas Cantilupe in my book, *Love in the Roses*, I should probably explain... This is housed in Hereford Cathedral. He had many miracles attributed to him, mostly healing, and there was mention of him aiding fertility.

To go on pilgrimage was no mean feat. It could take around a year to complete. The roads were long and hard and often plagued by bandits. This is why they often travelled in groups — safety in numbers, and all that.

Phew, that was a lot on religion! But I did say it was important to medieval folks, right? So, your character/s will probably need to know at least some of this stuff. Even if it's just so you know what vices they have.

Religion is maybe one of the biggest things that will make your character's opinions different from your own. Trying to understand their perspective on this will really help you get into their mindset.

Writing Prompt – Religion

The bell rings for Mass. Is your character in attendance?

- Is your MC religious (which religion)?
- How often do they attend church?
- Are there any saints days their village particularly celebrate?
- Can they see/take part in any pageants or festivities?
- Are they going to get married?
- Which sins are they going to commit (& will they do penance)?

TELLING THE TIME

Please note, that the years were based on the **Julian Calendar**. The Gregorian Calendar was introduced in 1582. And that the year's date/number did not change until 25th March (until 1752), yet 1st January was still called New Year's Day.

Fun fact: 25th March was the Feast of the Annunciation of the Blessed Virgin (aka Lady Day) – nine months before Christmas Day (*nudge nudge*). It makes **Sep**tember, **Oct**ober, **Novem**ber and **Dec**ember make sense (being 7th-10th months then)! And is also why, even now, the UK's tax year begins on 6th April (date got shifted along with the Gregorian calendar) – the tax man therefore missed 0 revenue.

The Julian calendar used the sun (noon) as the starting point. Leap years were 366 days; originally, 6 months of 30 days, 6 months of 31 days. February was the last month of the year; 29 days in leap years, 28 in others. The 1 day taken from February was added to August. The specific method applied, created a 1 day shift every 128 years.

Right, that's the calendar sorted.

In an era before watches or even really clocks as we know them, how did one know what time it was?

For a start, there were **canonical hours** which dictated prayer times. The three major hours were Matins, Lauds and Vespers. The minor hours were Terce, Sext, None/s and Compline. The church bell/s would be rung at each of these hours.

The length of hours varied according to the amount of light. e.g. in 12th century London, **matins** (first light) was rung at: 2.30am at midsummer, 5am at the equinox, but 6.40 am during midwinter.

Similarly, **vespers** (last light), was rung at: 7pm at midsummer, 5pm at the equinox, but 3pm during midwinter.

For *Love Habit*, I laboriously worked out roughly when that was the equivalent to in our hours (to schedule the monks' days). The complication being it was based on *daylight*, as previously stated. Well, this varies greatly both seasonally and regionally. There was a summer schedule and a winter one. Based on when sunrise and sunset (before Daylight Savings / BST!) in Kent, one could guesstimate:

Summer			
Office	Time (roughly)	Duration	
Matins/Night Office/Nocturns	02:00	1 hour	
Loo break	03:00		
Lauds (a later portion of Vigils from dawn)	03:30	30 mins	Sunrise - 03:30
Reading	04:00		
Prime (early morning, the first hour of daylight)	04:30	30 mins	
Breakfast (bread & ale)	05:00		
Work	05:30		
Terce (third hour)	06:30	30 mins	
Mass	07:00	30 mins	
Chapter Meeting	07:30		
High Mass	08:00	1 hour	
Work/Reading	09:00		
Sext (sixth hour)	09:30	30 mins	
Work/Reading	10:00		
Midday Meal "dinner"	11:30	1 hour	
Nones (ninth hour)	12:30	30 mins	
Work/Reading	13:00		
Vespers (sunset)	19:00	30 mins	
Supper	19:30	30 mins	Sunset - 20:15
Compline (end of the day before retiring)	20:00	30 mins	

Winter (from 1 November till Easter)			
Office	Time (roughly)	Duration	
Matins/Night Office/Nocturns	00:00	1 hour	
Loo break then back to sleep	01:00		
Reading	06:00		
Breakfast (bread & ale)	07:30		
Lauds (a later portion of Vigils from dawn)	08:00	30 mins	Sunrise - 07:59
Work	08:30		
Prime (early morning, the first hour of daylight)	09:00	30 mins	
Work/Reading	09:30		
Terce (third hour)	10:30	30 mins	
Midday Meal "dinner"	11:00		
Mass	12:00	30 mins	
Chapter Meeting	12:30		
Sext (sixth hour)	13:00	30 mins	
Work	13:30		
Nones (ninth hour)	14:00	30 mins	
Work/Reading	14:30		
Vespers (sunset)	15:00	30 mins	
Supper	15:30	30 mins	Sunset - 15:52
Warming Room/calefactory (winter)	16:00		
Compline (end of the day before retiring)	18:00	30 mins	
Sleep	18:30		

Table of Monks' Schedule, Summer & Winter, as worked out by TL Clark

Now, some towns had started to get fancy astronomical clocks, but these were still rare. So, nobody was inviting friends around to lunch at 1 o'clock, mate.

There were **sundials**. Apparently, some peasants even had them on the bottom of their shoes. They'd take the shoe off, face the sun and see where the shadow of the heel fell; clever! Sundials remained a stalwart of time-telling until watches, really. They are amazingly accurate, after all.

Another nifty device was the **coil candle**. These could be used as a kind of clock because it always took the same amount of time until a winding of the coil candle was burned. So, it was a sort of timer and source of light in one. But these would have been expensive, so again, another thing for the rich people.

In the 14th century, the **hourglass** seems to have emerged. You know, the thing with sand in. And they became rather popular.

But what about an **alarm clock**? There were some people, such as the sacrist in the monastery, who HAD to rise at all hours to ring the bell so others knew what time it was. Well, there was the less reliable 'cockcrow' method, used by the Romans. One thinks of this as early dawn. However, cockerels crow throughout the night. And based on the one on the farm I stayed at, some of them just never shut up at all. And even if it had cried at the right moment, it wouldn't have been early enough for matins.

If one was awake, you could look up at the **stars** and judge from their location. But that's not going to rouse you from sleep. Maybe more a good check to make sure you've got it right?

So, we turn to the **water clock**. These apparently first appeared in Ancient Egypt around 1200 BC. But they only started to appear in Europe from 11th century. There was no dial/face on these. It was just a weight on a rope which turned an axle that hit a bell on a rod. One could vary the length of the rope to ensure it struck at the appropriate hour. Fine until it got cold and the water froze!

Admittedly, there were a few **mechanical clocks** from the 13th century. They were weight-driven and had the ability to strike a chime. And were the product of Islamic and European science brains. For the first time, the day was split into 24 equal parts. But they tended to be large and expensive.

Fun fact: One could not actually claim time cost you money in the Middle Ages. Merchants were not able to charge fees on unpaid debt as that was akin to charging interest, which was illegal for most of the era. Time belonged to God!

Book of Hours

A Books of Hours was a simplified version of the Breviary. A prayer book, to be read at certain times of the day - the canonical hours as explained above. They were shorter to fit around the lives of the laity, and did not change with the day or liturgical season like the complex offices recited by the clergy (from psalters).

They were often illuminated (ornately decorated). Frequently shown in the hands of fine women in portraits, but were cherished by both men and women, from middle class upwards. But plainer versions were available for the 'lower orders'.

Almost every Book of Hours contains the two most common prayers to the Virgin Mary; the *Obsecro te* ('I beseech thee') and *O intemerata* ('O chaste one').

NB The term 'Book of Hours' has been fairly recently applied. At the time, they may have been called a **primer**.

Also, if you ever want a giggle, look up **'marginalia'** from psalters or books of hours. These were the images beautifully drawn. By monks! And first led me to pondering why the Religious had such a bottom fixation (hence *Love Habit* was born!). There are some hilarious images out there.

Writing Prompt – Time

Your character gets invited to a friend's house for some business chat.

- What time is it?
- Do they travel by moonlight?
- Are they awake at the crack of dawn?

MONEY

Your character, at some point, will probably need to buy something. Do you remember a world before online shopping? What about pre-decimalisation? Yeah, we're going back to pounds, shillings and pence. So let me break it down a bit.

Standard coins in use in the 15th century

- Groat (four pence)
- Half groat
- Half penny
- Farthing (one quarter of a penny)

Units used in accounting but not actual coins:

- Pound (two hundred and forty pence/20s)
- Mark (one hundred and sixty pence/two thirds of a pound/13s 4d)
- Shilling (twelve pence)

l, s, d = pounds, shillings and pence

Latin abbreviations for:

- liber
- solidus
- (Roman) denarius

The **gold noble**; before **1464** was valued at 6s 8d.

However, after that, it became the rose-noble or ryal and was valued at 10s. At the same time, the gold coin, the angel, was issued, valued at 6s 8d.

Later, Henry VII created a gold coin in 1489; the first sovereign, valued at 20s.

Weird fact: Although prices could be referred to in shillings, it wasn't actually a coin in the medieval era. It was Henry VII again who brought these in but called it the testoon (large head)!?

Fun comes back in the late 18th century, when folk started calling shilling coins 'bob'.

A few other coins appeared under different rulers, but I don't want to over-complicate things.

Coins were hammered, therefore had a rough appearance. Milled/machine-made (smooth) coins didn't appear until the 17th century.

So, **what would all this buy you?**

Staff Wages

Running a household was costly. Wages and livery soon mounted up (more details to follow under 'servants').

Almost half of one's annual income may have been spent on maintaining the household.

Quarter Days were when rents and taxes would be collected, servants hired at mop fairs and legal matters attended to. They fell on:

- ✠ **Lady Day** – 25th March / The Feast of the Anunciation / spring equinox
- ✠ **Midsummer** – 24th June / the Nativity of St John the Baptist / summer solstice
- ✠ **Michaelmas** – 29th September / Michaelmas / autumn equinox
- ✠ **Christmas** – 25th December / winter solstice

General Purchases (a rough guide)

So, your character wants to go shopping. What could they buy?

- Rent; merchant's house – L33-66 per year
- Knight's armour (complete) – L16 6s 8d
- Gown (fashionable lady's) – L10
- Ready-made armour (probably from Milan) - L8 6s 8d
- Mail (armour) – 100s
- A book – L1
- 6 silver spoons – 14s
- Gold brooch – 13s
- An ox – 13s
- Saffron – 12s per lb
- A cow – 10s
- Gold ring – 7s
- Rent; cottage – 5s per year
- Tunic (decent) – 5s
- 80 lbs cheese – 3s 4d
- Spices – 1-3s per lb
- A sheep – 1s
- Linen – 1s
- Wine (good) – 8d per gallon (1 gallon is 8 pints / 4.5 litres)
- Tunic (peasant) – 36d
- Hat (posh) – 10d
- Shirt (peasant) – 8d
- Pair of gloves – 7d
- Candles (wax) – 6.5d
- A goose – 6d
- Sword (poor) – 6d
- Shoes (posh) – 4d
- Candles (tallow) – 1.5d
- Ale – 1d per gallon
- A lamb – 1d
- 2 chickens – 1d
- A dozen eggs – ha'penny

Writing Prompt – Money

It's time to go shopping – yippee!

- How much money does your MC have?
- Are they going to buy something nice?
- How long do they have to save up to buy a little treat?

SERVANTS

Let us look at the wealthy. One sees references to the 'household'. This did not just mean the family in charge. Household accounts managed all costs associated with running the house. This included staff who were often provided for in wills. There was a co-dependency which created a strong bond.

Castles, palaces and great houses needed people to run them, of course.

Fun fact: Did you know the vast majority of servants in a medieval household were male? Washing, cooking, cleaning - all men. It was not uncommon for the only female to be the lady's maid.

Household Staff

Servants of the household were given board and lodging as well as a clothing allowance which included a badge/emblem to signify whose household they belonged to — all of this was the livery. Therefore, their actual wages were minimal.

- **Clergy** - sang mass and said prayers
- **Steward** - supervised the running of the courts, made local appointments, procurement, negotiated tenancy agreements, accompanied auditors to check annual accounts, and logistics
- **Chamberlain** - matters of the chamber; looked after the family chest (kept at the end of the bed and contained family deeds & money), ensured the chamber was warm & comfy, took charge of the liveries and clothes (which were often decorated with jewels - kept in the garderobe for extra protection from lice)
- **Chaplain** (in larger households; the Chancellor) - presided over daily Mass, attended to the spiritual welfare of the household. Had his own clerks.
- **Scribes / Clerks** - dealt with correspondence, kept records of the estates and business matters
- **Squires** - lesser nobility companions, would accompany on travels
- **Musicians** - music was an important part of entertainment, along with (often travelling) actors, troubadours, acrobats and jesters
- **Valet (aka Groom)** - collected purchases and perhaps prepped meals, assisted the chamberlain,

helped the lord to get dressed. Well-born but a lower servant. Rhymes with mallet.

- **Young Men** - accompanied masters/mistresses on journeys, ran errands and took messages
- **Kitchen Staff** - Cook was in charge, plus any/all of: a pastry cook, saucier, baker, butcher, waferer, fruiterer, spit-boys and scullions
- **Butler** - part of the kitchen staff, but worth noting: in charge of the buttery (store room for alcoholic beverages), and served said alcoholic beverages
- **Men** - to tend horses and traction animals (not known as grooms as those were valets)
- **Maintenance Servants** - looked after living quarters; window cleaning, washing floors, keeping fires/candles/rushlights alight
- **"Boys"** - lowest servants
- **Additional Staff** – particularly if there were frail and elderly to take care of, or sometimes extras were hired in during high demand e.g. banquets

- **Bailiff** - not of the inner house, but important. He collected rents and was a representative of the manor. Lowlier than the steward. Basically, oversaw the farming part of the estate; ensured livestock were looked after, thievery was minimal, oversaw sheep shearing, bought in items such as nails, tar and iron, sold wood and skins, decided when livestock should be bought/sold.

- **Receivers** - officials who oversaw financial matters for a group of distant manors (especially those leased for cash)

Interestingly, it was often the lady of the house (the lord's wife) who oversaw the 'inner/diet (household) accounts'. Expenditure such as food and clothing i.e. the day-to-day admin and financial matters.

Whilst the lord was more concerned with warfare, politics and the acquisition and protection of property - the 'outer accounts'.

And when her husband was away or died, she would oversee everything.

Yes, there was a steward to do this, but the owners would have to oversee these things and decide who was worthy of a seat at their table.

Livery (Clothing Allowance)

A typical landowner gave x24 householders eight yards of green cloth at just under 1s per yard. Lesser servants were given lesser amounts. But the total came to £8 for summer livery. This could amount to £36 for the annual clothing livery.

Once or twice per year, the household servants would be called, when this livery cloth would be given and wages paid, in person, by the lord or lady of the house. This personal contact would often come with a private word to each staff member, and was an important re-enforcement of gratitude as well as authority.

Labourers

Outside the household, a manor would have permanent agricultural workers.

Pay for these folk probably would have included grain etc. too.

Amounts in brackets are in shillings, and were the recommended wages according to the **1388 Ordinance of Labourers** which was reaffirmed by Parliament in 1349 (ooh, workers' rights!). The others, I've not been able to find accurate wages for.

- Grangers
- Reapers
- Mowers
- Swineherds and female labourers (6s)
- Herdsmen - ox or cow (6s 8d)
- Plough team members (7s)
- Carters (10s)
- Shepherds (10s)
- Blacksmiths
- Harvest reeve – a supervisor (15s)
- Bailiff – the big boss (20s)

Any extra work would be contracted to casual labourers.

You then had craftsmen / skilled labour:

(L being £)

- ❖ Master Mason / Carpenter – 53s (L4)
- ❖ Thatcher – 37s (L3)
- ❖ Weaver – 32s (L2)

Blacksmiths are difficult to pin down; I suspect if they lived on an estate, they collected some wages but could earn considerably more if they made items such as weaponry or armour. And some were probably fully independent. They did belong to guilds, so were skilled craftsmen. The bulk of their work was making pots and utensils, generally. But on an estate, making/repairing farming tools would likely be their main occupation.

The rent collector (or harvest reeve) would collect the rents from tenant farmers. Most of these tenants would be expected to contribute some boon work during harvest, but then get paid in cash or commodity rents the rest of the time.

Part-time tenant farmers may have been expected to shoe traction animals, dig ditches, herd animals, cart hay, produce/maintain farm buildings/implements and assist with arable cultivation.

Incidentally, the **peasant women partook in cottage industries** such as wool/flax spinning and even brewing ale. Or helped to produce leather, metal or textile wares.

Also, if they did manage to get employed in any of the above positions, they were paid lower wages (*rolls eyes*).

Writing Prompt – Servants

Work, work, work – it's never done. The house has to be kept clean, the fires must be lit and food must be prepared.

- Is your MC a servant?
- Or do they have servants?
- What duties must they perform?

WRITING

A quick note on writing. For, in the above list of servants, one may observe a 'scribe or clerk'. These employees clearly still existed. However, it did not mean everyone was entirely illiterate. And by the end of the 15th century, household scribes were dwindling.

To put this into context, we need to look at the English language used in speech.

Language

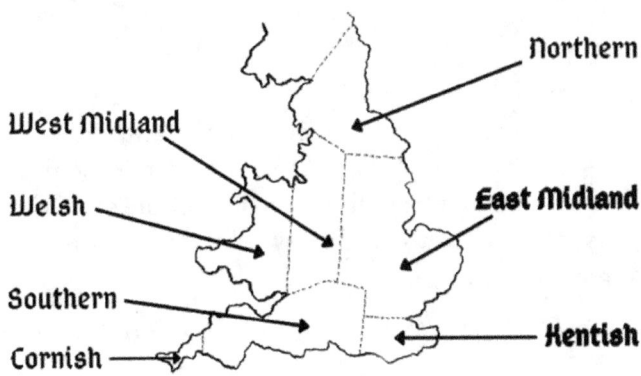

Fig 2- Map of medieval English dialects, drawn by Angeline Trevena

From around 1066, the Norman Conquest, language had gradually **shifted from Old English** (with its Germanic dialects which later gained Norse influence) **through to Middle English** with its Norman French leanings. This also saw **the Great Vowel Shift**.

e.g. Chaucer wrote in Middle English in the 14th century.

On top of this, there were many different **dialects** spoken (see previous diagram).

As a spoken language, French dominated amongst the nobles from around 1066, and government from around 1250. Only falling from mainstream use in the 14th century.

English had been the language of the conquered Anglo-Saxons. And it had quietly endured. So, by the mid-fifteenth century, English managed to reassert its dominance.

What I'm saying is, **French, Latin and English were all fairly commonplace in 15th century England**.
It was a multilingual nation.

Now, if we think about the printing press, the East Midlands dialect aka Chancery Standard or **standardised English**, started to crop up with its introduction to England in 1476 (late 15th century). So, this was not yet the everyday language used in writing by ordinary folk. It would take time to spread and change.

e.g. William Shakespeare wrote in Early Modern English in the 16th century.

Most religious and legal documents were written in Latin. But at least some letters were written in English during the 15th century; there is the collection of correspondence known as *the Paston Letters* which shows this nicely.

Another quick note on language; use the spelling of the country your book is set in. The UK has weirdly different spelling and dialect from our American cousins. As you're reading this book, I'm going to assume you're writing about England, so keep it English.

Hardly anyone speaks Middle English now, so do feel free to write in Modern English. However, try to avoid modern slang/terms e.g. OK or alright.

I'll provide some fun slang in the final section of this book.

Reading

There were such things as **reading primers**; printed booklets teaching the alphabet. These had apparently been around for a while. But seem to have grown in popularity in the early 1500s (16th century) when they could be bought for a penny. I'm pretty sure the printing press also helped with this. And there were other ways to display this as well.

So, **maybe more people could read than we give them credit for**. After all, medieval schools did teach reading. But for most people, this was more for correct pronunciation as opposed to understanding/comprehension of the text. As well as the Latin alphabet, they would have learned simple prayers e.g. the Pater Noster, the Ave, and the Creed.

And writing was a different beast again.

So, as a reminder; **the vast majority of documents were still written in Latin** during the 15th century. Certainly, household accounts and legal documents were. Ah!

Well, it was the rich boys who got sent to grammar schools where Latin was taught. As the 'lady of the manor' had to keep ordinance of the accounts, one must gather they were taught rudimentary reading and writing. But we will explore education more fully soon.

Arguably, the place you'd find the greatest quantity of writers was still in the monasteries.

Writing Implements

Paper

Vellum or parchment was used for handwriting. (Vegans skip ahead!).

- ❖ Vellum was made of calfskin (and was more expensive)
- ❖ Parchment was made of sheep or goatskin

I won't go into the gory detail of how these were made; it's nasty and unnecessary detail.

Suffice it to say that either form of paper was incredibly durable, and shockingly, it wasn't until 2017 that the UK decided to stop using it to write our laws on!

Scribes would mark the pages with horizontal and vertical lines. From the 14th century, this may have been done with a **plummet** (pencil), or a **metal stylus** made of lead or silver may have been used.

The pens were in the form of a **quill**. I'm going to assume you know these are made of the (flight) feather of a large bird. But they were quite tricky to write with. One could really only write with downward strokes. And each letter had to be broken down into several strokes.

Fonts

Different forms of **lettering** emerged.

- ❖ **Textura** – aka book hand, Gothic script or *literal textualis*; pen lifted after every stroke, upright, angular, very formal but slow. Used mainly by monks for formal and expensive books. During the 14th and 15th century, it was used almost exclusively for liturgical or devotional manuscripts.

- ❖ **Anglicana** – aka charter hand, court hand or *cursiva antiquior*; a form of cursive script; more rounded, pen could stay on the page. It seems to have started in the 13th century. This was a quicker method to meet the increasing demand for cheaper books.

- ❖ **Secretary** – aka script; a simplified, flowing, looping cursive hand which was used from the late 14th century. Used for business, personal and literary manuscripts.

Ink

Scribes usually produced their own ink. Sourced from natural products (again, I'm sparing you the details), most recipes included lamp-black mixed with gum or iron gall. And was held in an inkhorn on a stand beside their desk.

But they also needed colours, especially for those pretty, illuminated manuscripts.

Common colours (and shades):

- Red – murrey, sanguin, scarlet or vermillion
- Blue – azurite, celestine, inde, pers, ultramarine, woad
- Yellow – carsey, crocus, isabelle, jaune
- Green – lincoln, Verdigris, verdulet
- Brown – brun, burn, burnetta (lighter), russet, tawny

The pigment most commonly used to paint **flesh colours** was **'light cinabrese'** (Venetian red).

Fun fact: Colours which had **not yet** been named; **orange** (not until 1512) and **pink** (a late-comer of the 17th century). Pink was referred to as 'rosy'.

If you think of the bird 'the robin redbreast', it does, in fact, have orange on its little self – named before orange became a named colour.

If a scribe made a mistake, they'd have to scrape it off with a **knife**. They'd also need that knife to sharpen their quill.

And **sand** would be used to absorb excess ink.

Writing practice was done on **wax tablets**. Parchment was far too precious to be used for anything but 'best handwriting'.

One could warm the wax then use the flat end of the stylus to erase the writing. Or heat it up a bit more and tilt the tablet from side to side to clear a lot of text (a bit like an Etch A Sketch).

Books were made up of sections (quires) which were assembled in the correct order then sewn together with leather cords/thongs. Wooden boards (usually oak) would then be placed either side and sometimes covered with leather which could be stamped with fancy designs. Metal mounts were occasionally also added.

Symbology

To be honest, I wasn't quite sure where to add this little bit of info, but here seems as good a place as any. The medieval era was fond of symbology.

In general:
- ❖ Red carnations represented true love
- ❖ Viola odorata (sweet violet) was a symbol of humility
- ❖ Cemetery gardens, which tended to be very similar to generic orchards, acted as a symbol of Heaven and Paradise
- ❖ Partridges "forgot their sex" so symbolized homosexuality

But then you had the **bestiary** - a descriptive or anecdotal treatise on various real or mythical kinds of animals, with a moralizing tone. It contained things such as:
- ❖ **Fox** – sly; a trickster that would roll over on its back and pretend to be dead, luring unsuspecting birds into its midst.
- ❖ **Goose** – vigilant; can smell the odour of man better than any other animal can
- ❖ **Hare** – fear; a timid beast that runs fast
- ❖ **Lion** – king of beasts; resurrection. According to the bestiary, lion cubs are born dead, and after three days their parents literally breathe life into them.
- ❖ **Partridge** – deceit; a bird that steals other birds' eggs
- ❖ **Unicorns** – purity/Christ/strength; a wild, untameable beast that could be captured only by a maiden in the woods.
  – also symbolised incarnation. Later, came to symbolise courtly love.

Then of course, you had **emblems** worn by the military e.g. King Richard III had a white boar emblem/badge/device, for instance.

This may have also been worn as a badge by the household servants btw – remember I mentioned them? I believe this was a sew-on patch type thing.

There will be more on coats of arms & heraldry in the 'Knights And Weaponry' section shortly.

Writing Prompt – Writing

Someone sits down to write a letter. Is it your MC?

- Can your MC read or write?
- Does this help or hinder?
- Do they employ a scribe?
- Is writing part of their daily life?

EDUCATION

Education was seemingly low on the list of priorities for your average Joe – what do you want with book learning when you got to tend the fields?

But, as briefly discussed in the 'writing' section above, literacy by the 14th century was rising. At least, in terms of being able to sound out syllables and words in Latin, even if they couldn't understand them.

Most formal education was reserved for the boys. And even then, only if they were destined to become part of the clergy, law, medicine, or business.

The most learned of the land were the Religious. Ergo, they were predominantly in charge of education.

Fun fact: monks didn't only study the Bible.

Myriad subjects were covered in multiple languages, both theological and philosophical. Classical literature/philosophy was studied e.g. Aristotle, Plato, and Cicero.

But also subjects such as law, history, music, science, arithmetic, geometry, astronomy, astrology, the occult, magic, alchemy, medicine and herbalism.

They translated a lot of texts from Arabic and Greek.

Types of Schools

- ✠ Parish church schools
- ✠ Cathedral schools
- ✠ Chantry schools in cathedrals
- ✠ Monastic schools
- ✠ Grammar schools
- ✠ Endowed / public schools
- ✠ Guild schools
- ✠ Free schools
- ✠ Almonry schools

Small, informal schools seem to have existed in **parish** churches, but precious little can be found out about them. Perhaps rudimentary reading was taught here, certainly reading of the Psalms. Or the priests wanted to encourage their congregation to aspire to a career in the church, so gave them basic instruction?

NB Actual village schools seem not to have emerged until after 1500.

Cathedral schools were set up to train priests, but expanded to teach sons of nobles who were destined for high positions of church, state or business. The teachers were of the clergy. And yes, they would've had to sing in the choir. Canterbury, Hereford, London, Rochester, Winchester and York had such establishments.

e.g. The King's School, Canterbury – founded 597AD by St Augustine himself, making it possibly the oldest continually operated school in the world. It was only named "The King's School" after the Dissolution, presumably to ingratiate Henry VIII's favour which clearly worked. It's still a public school now.

Chantry schools are pretty much what they sound like. Chantries were set up by wealthy patrons so priests could sing masses for the dearly beloved in perpetuity (forever). However, this didn't take up all of their time, so the priests were then 'encouraged' to undertake teaching too. Education was in the form of both grammar and singing. Because the chantry was already funded, there were generally no school fees charged.

e.g. Chantry Chapel of All Souls, Higham Ferrers, Northamptonshire – which became a grammar school after the Reformation and lasted until 1906.

Monastic schools were held within the monastery. Monks taught here. By the 15th century, they were largely seen as preparatory schools for would-be monks. Students were taught to read and write Latin.

Lessons in scripture, theology, arithmetic and chanting were included.

Secular texts did also exist, including 'the Classics' (y'know, Ancient Greek and Roman stuff, such as the poems and philosophy of Titus Lucretius Carus, Marcus Fabius Quintilianus, Aristotle, Virgil and Homer).

Herbalism, science and medicine were also important subjects.

Monks were incredibly learned people.

Boys were most frequently sent to **grammar** schools, age 7 to 14. University would possibly have followed. These charged attendance fees. As well as the basic subjects, pupils were also taught Latin grammar and comprehension; vital for anyone going into a profession where documents were handled e.g. lawyer or clerk.

e.g. The Royal Grammar School Worcester, was originally founded around 685AD and is still going.

And Thetford Grammar School, Norfolk which may date back to a similar time.

The **endowed** schools were **public schools** i.e. students came from all over the land, not just locally. They tended to be in towns, and there are records of such in Cambridge, King's Lynn, Lewes, Nottingham and Shrewsbury. These were the elite, boarding schools for the very rich.

e.g. Eton which was founded in 1440 by King Henry VI.

Guilds provided schools for apprentices, obviously more concerned with teaching the skills of their trade. These then evolved into **burgher schools**, encompassing a broader range of students, and sometimes merging with chantry schools.

e.g. Merchant Taylors' School in London started as a guild school (in a manor house) in 1561. Yes, later than the 15th century, but it's still a public school now, so thought it interesting to include.

I also find it fascinating that there were other schools provided by the same company: a grammar school at Macclesfield in 1502, one at St. Mary's Wike in Cornwall in 1508, and Wolverhampton Grammar School in 1508 which maintains it's company links even now.

Also, when 'the king who I don't care to name again', demolished all the monasteries in the 16th century, it brought down almost all of the education system along with it. (*claps sarcastically*) "Well done. Great job, Your Majesty!" (*rolls eyes, shakes head*). Thankfully, the burgher schools were independent from the religious community, so survived and helped save some others - actual yay them! Hospitals were endangered too btw. ^Genius^!

By the end of the 14th century, **free** (charity) schools started to emerge. Monies were donated by the wealthy, so the schools didn't have to charge for tuition.

Similarly, there were **almonry** schools in some larger monasteries around the same time. The almoner took some of the donations made to their monastery and paid for **places at the cathedral school** and provided for board and lodging — a scholarship. Boys from the age of 10 who could sing and read could then access this prized education.

e.g. Eton College was originally set up as a free school so that 70 poor boys could then go on to study at King's College, Cambridge. Err, so, it's not run that way now and hasn't been for a while. It's long since become one of the most prestigious, elite, public, boarding, all-boys schools in the land, although it does still offer 70 scholarships each year.

Also interesting to look at (but established after the medieval era), is Christ's Hospital School, Horsham. In 1552, this charitable school formed in what was once the monastery of the Grey Friars on Newgate Street. Pupils still wear the Tudor-style uniform including distinctive yellow socks.

If a boy went on to **university**, it was to learn business studies, or liberal arts. They could then seek further study of medicine, canon or civil law, or theology.

e.g. University of Oxford (founded 1096), University of Cambridge (founded 1209), the wonderfully named College of the Valley Scholars, Salisbury (1262-1542)

There was, of course, one important area I've not discussed here – the **military**. Knights had their own training, as will be covered in their very own section, because they were just that special.

Education for Girls

Often, girls' education is dismissed as something that was just done at home by their mothers. However, as well as that option, they could also attend elementary schools, and nunneries, or via employment and apprenticeship. In the royal court, it was even possible to join a classroom there.

Depending on their socioeconomic status, girls were taught various subjects, including: practical skills, reading comprehension, and social accomplishments.

Perhaps reading for wealthy girls was encouraged and developed through prayer books, books of hours or psalters. However, French and English would have been learned as well as Latin.

But this wasn't necessarily the extent of their learning. There is evidence to suggest that some noble girls were also instructed in the arts, including: arithmetic, archery, astronomy, the classics, decorum, geometry, hunting, music, philosophy, riding, tapestry, writing and theology.

Wealthy girls would be expected to run their household accounts once married, don't forget.

If a young woman was intended to gain a trade, she would have needed to be able to read and write. Possible work options included: book binding, notary work, shopkeeping or textiles.

By the end of the 15th century, a young woman could even become a schoolmistress.

As young boys aiming to enter monastic life learned Latin, so too did young girls seeking to become nuns. Therefore, it was taught in the nunnery schools. Interestingly, there is an account stating the correspondence between bishops and nunneries was written mainly in French in the 14th century, but then English in the 15th century.

e.g. St Hilda at Whitby Abbey gathered a magnificent library in the 7th century, and ensured the nuns had a high level of education. All convent schools were within nunneries, so were destroyed during the Dissolution, I'm afraid.

Livre pour l'enseignement de ses filles (Chevalier de La Tour Landry) by Geoffroy IV de la Tour Landry – was written in 1372. But was translated into English by William Caxton as *The Book of the Knight of the Tower* in 1483.

In the preface, Caxton added that it was intended not just for noble girls but for all classes. There was a growing demand for such instructional books, particularly among the burgher class.

This particular one served as a tutorial for De la Tour Landry's daughters on proper behaviour when visiting the royal court. The author was a widower knight, who wished to warn his daughters of the smooth-talking courtiers who could potentially disgrace them and embarrass the family. He took a strong moral stance against the behaviour of his peers and warned his daughters about the dangers of vanity.

So, do you now feel better educated about medieval education?

Writing Prompt – Education

What do you want with book learning, anyway? Does your MC have ideas above their station?

- Is your MC at school (or did they go to one)?
- What do/did they learn?
- Is your book set in an educational establishment?
- What are the teachers like?

LAW

Why does this make me shudder? Maybe I'm just imagining the villainous sheriff of Nottingham. However, the law was also an important part of medieval life.

Law Enforcement Roles

Sheriff

Starting with this office since I've just mentioned it; the role held great importance. From around 1077, men of high rank and power could be nominated (their names offered to the king) to be appointed sheriff (or shire-reeve) for one year. He could then *not* be re-appointed for three years afterwards.

His duty was to investigate allegations of crime in his shire, conduct investigations, try lesser cases and detain those accused of greater offences so they may be tried.

Should villagers fail to catch a criminal, the sheriff could call upon a *posse comitatus* (a posse) – a group of local men aged 15 or over, to catch them, no matter how far they ran.

He was also responsible for collecting rents and revenues within his district. He would have to pay any shortfall of those - ouch!

And he had to host visiting judges and dignitaries. It could all be very costly. And yet, a great honour. There were many men who tried to avoid it due to the cost implications, but if you were chosen you could not refuse.

Justice of the Peace

In 1327, there was an act which brought in the Justice of the Peace. This "good and lawful man" would be elected or appointed by means of a commission. His role was to actually to guard the peace in his region. There were typically eighteen per county. The contract stipulates he should, "bind over unruly persons to be of good behaviour". They were there more for prevention than punishment.

They conducted arraignments in all criminal cases and tried misdemeanours. They were actually quite important and useful people.

However, it was an **unpaid** office! They were typically members of the gentry, and (*coughs*) may have been more concerned with the prestige.

NB The JP is the origin of what we now know as magistrates.

Coroners

There have indeed been coroners since 1194. Each county had four of them. And they were responsible for investigating suspicious/sudden deaths, and reporting their findings to the sheriff.

Constables

Not officially police yet – they didn't come along until the 19th century. But they do seem to have borrowed the term from these medieval folk.

Parish constables in medieval England were upstanding local men who held the office for one year. They were responsible for raising the alarm (the literal *hue and cry*) in case of any criminal activity – catch that criminal!

Reporting to these chaps were the **watchmen** of the town who roamed the streets at night, keeping a beady eye on suspicious people, handing them over to the constable if needs be. Known collectively as 'the watch'.

It took a whole village to police itself. Every person was expected to watch one another's backs, and jump upon any wrongdoing.

We then move on to a high-level view of **the court system** itself…

Judicial Courts

Look, this can all get a bit confusing, and you probably won't need it, so I'm just going to give the basics.

Often, the first port of call was the **Manorial or Manor Court**. This was for the manor's tenants, and would typically deal with issues such as land disputes and petty crime; things the lord of the manor had jurisdiction over. It was the lowest court of the land.

This is where our magistrates' courts stemmed from.

Court Leet - this was more on a baronial level. A jury would sit, comprised often of twelve freehold tenants. Officers of the leet could be the likes of manorial stewards or bailiffs. It was a court of record and a place to protect the peace. They also became responsible for ensuring the good condition of watercourses, roads, paths and ditches. This court also sought to protect public rights and the use of common land and defended against the adulteration of food. The court leet would only sit a few times per year.

Church Courts
Of course, the Church had its own courts. Instead of a jury, they had priests who passed judgement. Not only could they try members of the clergy but also anyone accused of adultery, failing to attend church, gambling, heresy or blasphemy – vices which would offend God.

Priests could be tried at the Assizes, but only the Church could issue their punishment.

'**Benefit of Clergy'** was often claimed. For this would mean no death sentence could be passed. Well, of course, many criminals claimed this benefit who were not, in fact, clergymen. So, after 1351, there was a verse from the Bible (which came to be known as the 'neck verse'), they had to *read* as proof they were a man of the Church. Well, of course, seasoned yet illiterate criminals learned this verse off by heart just in case. Sorry ladies; no female clergy in medieval England so we never got this 'benefit'.

In 1576, Church courts could no longer try criminal cases under Benefit of Clergy, but it wasn't officially, completely abolished until 1827, in case you're wondering.

Claiming Sanctuary was still in force until 1624, when Henry VIII abolished it. Any felon could actually claim sanctuary in a church. Some churches even had a 'sanctuary knocker/ring' on their door – a person merely had to hold that in order to claim refuge. They then had up to forty days to decide whether to accept a trial or become an exile (flee the country forever).

Chancery - the start of appeals of Common Law (although it does make me imagine the drudgery of the system portrayed in the much later, Charles Dickens book, *Bleak House*)

The Royal Courts / The Assizes

These tried the most serious crimes; those which typically could **hold a death sentence**. After 1293, the judges travelled to each county two or three times per year to hold trials. Alarmingly, they found over half the cases 'not guilty'.

Hundred Courts, Quarter Sessions and Borough Courts

Each county/shire was divided into subsections – the hundreds. Each hundred had its own court which tried lesser crimes such as petty theft, assault, and poaching.

This evolved into the administration of law and the keeping of the peace. They were run by the Justice of the Peace and met four times per year (the quarter sessions).

Interestingly, in 1971, this effectively became the Crown Court we know today.

The King's Bench - as the name suggests, dealt with serious matters which needed to be brought before the king.

The Star Chamber - introduced in the late 15th century, lasting until the mid-17th century. It sat at the royal Palace of Westminster, and typically tried the very important people who had too much political power/influence to be tried by the lower courts. It dealt with civil and criminal matters. But became a bit big for its boots and was abused to inflict political oppression (*feigns shock*).

Fun fact: A woman could take another to court and sue her for being called a whore in medieval England.

This covers the legal system/courts as an overview.

Crime & Punishment

There were varying levels of crime.

Petty Crime

Petty crimes were lowkey things which inflicted minimal harm. These included thefts valuing less than 12d (around £50 in today's money), debtors or minor injuries to people/property.

These were mainly punishable by fines. If they were tried in the manorial court, the lord of the manor would receive the money, church courts fines went to the Church, whilst mayors and town officials received fines via the borough court, and the monarch would receive fines payable to the hundred courts and the quarter sessions.

Scolding was included as a petty crime under the Statutes of Westminster of 1275. It extended the Church's condemnations of "blasphemy, hypocrisy, rumour, lying, flattery, mocking of good people, and sowing of discord". Deemed as abusive or offensive speech in public, it was most often women accused of this public nuisance. If the manor court found someone guilty, the punishment was to be bound to a cucking stool (a sort of commode) and paraded through the town for public humiliation.

The **pillory or stocks** were used to punish those guilty of dishonesty (people not abiding by the laws of weights and measures, in particular), drunkenness, brawling and sedition. It was punishment by public humiliation; crowds would gather to mock the offender for anything from half an hour to a whole day. It would hurt mentally as well as physically.

The **pillory** was a wooden or metal frame set on a raised platform, and where the criminal's head and hands were held fast. Crowds would point and jeer at the offender. Now, it's unlikely anyone threw food at folk in these – it was too precious to waste. But if there was some rotten food, it's possible that was used. Mud and excrement were frequently flung. Maybe some offal or dead animals too.

However, if the person had offended the mob, they could find items such as stones or bricks being thrown at them. And yes, some people did die in the pillory.

The **stocks** held only the feet and were the more lenient. There were some places in the UK still using these in the 19th century!

Imprisonment tended to be more for holding folk awaiting trial. Or for short-term punishment of those convicted of minor crimes such as debt, forgery or failure to pay fines. Prisoners had to purchase their own food and bedding in gaol!

Vagrancy
The Act of 1383 (aka The Beggars Act) came into being following the Peasants' Revolt in 1381. The Black Death, as detailed elsewhere, led to labour shortages. Therefore, anyone seen being idle and/or roaming uselessly about in another town/village was punishable by law – these folk were known as vagrants. Every man was expected to stay and work in their village of origin.

The Act of 1388 added that villeins must carry letters patent explaining the purpose of their journey when travelling away from their home.

Offenders were punishable by the Justice of the Peace, Justices of Assize or the sheriff. And could face forced labour (perhaps confinement in a labour house) or imprisonment.

This was still in force throughout the 15th century and was even added to in 1495 under Henry VII.

Poaching

This is actually difficult to categorise. It rather depended on location. Some villages seem to have turned the other cheek when folk were accused of poaching – people have to eat, after all. They took pity on the poor.

However, some villages issued fines for those breaking 'forest laws'. Imprisonment, stocks and even whipping were sometimes used as deterrents. However, if one was caught stealing game from a royal forest, you would be in real trouble.

There were organised gangs hunting animals in large numbers for their fur and meat. These were obviously taken a lot more seriously.

Since the Normans, it was illegal to graze animals, cut down trees and hunt on common land. But the *death penalty* for poaching was revoked in 1217… and then reinstated in 1723.

Serious Crime

These were crimes which were likely to attract (*dern dern dern*) the death penalty.

Hanging was the form of execution for those guilty of burglary, murder or theft of goods worth over 12d. This helps explain the low imprisonment rates, right? You steal you die – don't do the crime if you can't…face the noose? No, no, I've got it: don't burgle the hoose if ye dinnae want the noose. I'm using humour to detract from the hideousness, clearly. Moving on…

Hanging, drawing and quartering was reserved for people who committed high treason i.e. trying to kill the monarch, or even counterfeiting / clipping coins.

It was a particularly nasty way to go. The person was hung, but not until dead. Whilst still alive, they were brought down from the noose and disembowelled before finally being chopped into four pieces.

Peine forte et dure (Law French for "forceful and hard punishment"), was another horrendous punishment, brought in by the Statute of Westminster in 1275. Like, truly appalling. Skip if squeamish!

It was used on those who refused to plead either guilty or innocent – holding silent was the person's way of trying to save their estate for their family, for if a person was tried and convicted, they surrendered their goods and estates to the crown. Staying silent seemed the better option, even if it did by itself infer guilt.

But what was it? After 1406, the silent suspect could be pressed to death by increasingly heavy weights being laid upon them – actually being crushed to death.

Before that, it was more imprisonment and starvation until they submitted a plea. It wasn't abolished until 1772! Although, we still use phrases such as, "You'd be hard pressed to find (x,y,z)" or "If pressed, I'd say…".

Burning was the punishment for heresy (not believing in the teachings of the Church) from around the 14th century as well as for those who committed petty treason.

NB The witch trials held much later did *not* burn witches, though – they hung them (generally).

For those seeking **Trial by Ordeal**, I'm happy to say this was **abolished** by the Pope in 1215 (England stopped in 1219!), so doesn't feature here, in the 15th century. It was grizzly; if you're interested look it up at your own risk.

Also, **Trial by Combat** had all but disappeared after the jury system was brought in. This was where the accused person would literally fight the one who accused him. The one not dead at the end was obviously proved innocent as God saved him!? Although, the last official judicial duel held in England occurred in 1492, it's unlikely to have occurred much in 15th century England so is best avoided.

NB No matter the crime, the rich could always buy their way out, either by hefty fines or by giving a parcel of land to the Crown or the Church.

Writing Prompt – Law

Ooh, someone's in trouble. Is it your MC? I knew them for a badun from the moment I saw them.

- Is your MC a law-abiding citizen?
- Do they hold a position of responsibility?
- Or are they a criminal?
- Are any punishments going to be issued?

CLOTHING / FASHION

After all that, I think we need something a bit more fun. Although, the law does crop up even here.

I once heard it said on a history programme (sorry, I can't remember which), that there is a change of fashion along with each change of monarch. On the whole, this seems to be a pretty good rule of thumb, historically.

Now, as we've seen, there were many changes of king in the 15th century. And yes, the changes of fashion are applicable to both men and women.

Can I get the obvious out of the way? The main difference between rich and poor at this time was not in the style, but more the **quality of material**.

Sumptuary Laws

Let us glimpse at the weird Sumptuary Laws – we need to know some of the constraints our characters face. But I don't want to dwell on them too much.

Edward III, in the 14th century, seems to have been the first English monarch to impose such restrictions on what one was permitted to wear. His statute denied anyone under the rank of knight from wearing fur. And also forbade the import of textiles from outside of the British Isles and the export of wool. Some surmise this was to put a cap on the cost of household liveries. But it does seem to have been done to support our wool industry.

In 1363, part of the laws determined that knights (and their families) with land worth 400 marks annually may wear whatever they wish, with the exclusion of weasel and ermine furs, or clothing of precious stones (except those worn in ladies' hair).

However, knights (and their families) with land worth 200 marks may not wear fabric over the worth of £4 in total. **No cloth of gold**, nor a cloak, mantle or gown lined with pure miniver, sleeves of ermine or any material embroidered with precious stones; women may not wear ermine or weasel-fur, or jewels except those worn in their hair.

In 1463, a further Act introduced by Edward IV, placed further clothing restrictions, determined by social class. Knights below the rank of lord were prohibited from wearing any cloth of gold, anything wrought with gold or sable fur, and no velvet upon velvet. Their wives and children must follow these rules as well, for any person in this category caught with prohibited items would forfeit 20 marks to the King for each and every offence.

People with an income of less than 40s per annum were not permitted to wear any item prohibited in the higher classes or fustian, bustian, any scarlet cloth (purple or red), nor any fur except black or white lamb. A fine of 40s would be issued to any disobeying this.

A slightly more amusing section of this one was the legislation against the wearing of long-toed shoes (**poulaines** aka Cracow). They had become longer than the entire length of the foot! This just sounds like a trip hazard to me, but hey, it was a thing. Those less than a lord were restricted to a 2-inch pike on their shoes or boots.

Fun fact: A 12th century Benedictine monk had exclaimed that people who wore pointed shoes "gave themselves up to sodomitic filth", and that young men who wore them also had "long luxurious locks like women," and "over-tight shirts and tunics".

Now, I would like to remind you that "sodomy" usually meant *any* sexual activity outside of procreation purposes within marriage. But, in this context, the monk did seem to be snubbing gay guys. Rude! However, that clearly stopped nobody as they were still being worn into the 16th century. And who can blame them? The image conjured up is rather yummy! I'm pretty sure a lot of people would find their pulses racing at such a sight.

Whilst I'm discussing shoes, let us explore **patten shoes** – they were worn over the top of other shoes so as to better avoid the deep mud and err... excrement in the roads. They were usually a wooden platformed sole with leather straps, and were worn between 14th and 18th centuries.

Ankle boots also became fashionable.

And pretty much all footwear was made of leather.

Back to the Sumptuary Laws themselves...

In 1483, they took things even further still. All persons in England except for the royal family were forbidden to wear gold or purple silk. Persons below the level of duke were not permitted to wear cloth of gold or tissue, and no one below a lord could wear plain cloth of gold.

Servants of husbandry/peasants were not allowed to wear any material which cost more than 2s for the broad yard.

NB These were all fairly hard to enforce. People will always wear what they want, punishment be damned.

General Fabrics

- Fur
- Leather
- Linen
- Silk
- Wool

Fur was used as a warm lining.

Leather was tough and hardwearing, so was usually used for belts and shoes.

Linen was light and smooth, so used mainly for undergarments. Importantly; cheap and easy to wash.

Silk (including velvet, purple and taffeta) was the most expensive and reserved for the nobles.

Wool (including scarlet) was used for its warmth and water resistance in outer garments.

Furs (skip if squeamish):

- **Red Squirrel** – imported from Russia or Scandinavia. Its winter white belly fur was especially prized. So, obviously expensive and popular.
- **Gris** – from the grey squirrel (which had a bluish-grey tint in winter). Again, expensive and popular.
- **Vair** – a variegated, checkered pattern made of squirrel belly furs
- **Ermine** – came from the white winter coats of stoats
- **Lettice** – from the snow weasel, so again white
- **Minever** – the white belly furs but with a little of the grey framing it, in rectangles. There was also 'pured minever' which was only the white bit, used for trimming garments.
- **Marten** - a brown fur from pine martens
- **Fox / Vulpes** – could be red, grey, black or white, and thick
- **Beaver** – Popular brown fur for hats, and lining surcotes or cloaks
- **Sable** – a black marten. Especially popular in the 15th century as darker colours rose in high-end fashion.
- **Otter** – very similar to martens
- **Fitch** – from the polecat, light to dark brown, and rose up to replace the dwindling squirrel market
- **Budge** – black or white lambskin for lining hoods
- **Coney** (Rabbit) / **Hare** – for the poorer folks

Ladies Headwear

The **steeple** (conical) **hennin** is perhaps the most commonly associated with the medieval period, thanks to movie princesses. However, they really only emerged from around 1430, according to some sources. And petered out by around 1490. So, yay for our 15th century characters!

From around 1250-1500, the **escoffion** was en vogue. A thick, circular woollen/felt/silk band was rolled and worn in a horn shape. Gauze or silk could then be draped over. This is also of the hennin family of headwear.

Beehive (shorter, squatter) and **butterfly hennins** (wider, split horns) also had their time. The latter arising in the mid-15th century.

I rather like the **crespine**; fine netting worn either side of the head attached to a circlet.

Whatever style of headwear a person chose, whether rich or poor, male or female, **one should always cover their hair**. This was a pious, religious stipulation.

In fact, in 1162, **prostitutes** were forbidden from wearing a veil lest they should be mistaken for someone with virtue.

Prostitutes also broke the law by cross-dressing as men; well, they did have the more form-fitting clothing. Tight hose, anyone? Between 1450—1553, in London alone, there were thirteen cases of women of ill-repute who were prosecuted for dressing as men (at least one for wearing a priest's gown). Their punishment was to be marched through the streets — maybe the angry mob they passed actually shouted, "Shame!"? They were then exiled.

The harlots of Southwark aka The Winchester Geese (so called because the Bishop of Winchester owned the stews/brothels in that area), were banned from wearing aprons.

In 1351, the City of London passed a law determining that "lewd women" must wear a **striped hood**, and refrain from lining or trimming their garments with fur. This may have been a practice adopted from Bristol. And it seems to have spread throughout the land.

As fascinating as all this is, we should probably refocus on everyday folk.

As the Middle Ages continued, the **hairlines** grew higher. Ladies were known to pluck their hairline and wear their hats further back. Bald was apparently a desirable look!?

From the 13th to 15th centuries, women wore **wimples** (or gorgets). This should be worn over the chin. Unlike today's nuns who generally wear it under.

The **coif** was worn by men and women. A simple, linen bonnet/cap, usually tied under the chin. The 15th century rich folk tended to only wear these as nightcaps. The poor would keep it as daywear under other headwear.

Outer Garments

Oddly, ladies' gowns/dresses didn't undergo much of a change. It was more their headwear.

There was usually a woollen **kirtle** (or cotte) worn over a **chemise**. A noblewoman's chemise may have been made of linen or silk. Sometimes, women wore a houppelande or surcote but in a different style to those worn by men.

An **overgown** was then worn over these. The underlayers would have been washed more regularly. Whilst the top layer would have been made of the most expensive fabric they could manage and was decorated with fine jewels if they were rich.

Everybody would have had some form of **cloak** for colder weather. And usually made of wool. It really was quite good at keeping the rain off.

Colours

The choice of colour could hold significance. I may have used this symbology in *Love in the Roses* (*wink wink*).

- **Blue** - fidelity (and represents the Virgin Mary)
- **Green** - love
- **Grey** - sorrow
- **Red** (crimson) - privilege/power/blood of Christ
- **Yellow** - hostility (but also certain saints' days)

Men's Clothing

The male folk saw more variations. From long to short **houppelandes** (a sort of overcoat). This garment was fitted at the shoulders but with a flared skirt, and often belted. It replaced the tightly fitted surcoats of the 14th century. It was reserved for the nobility thanks to its extravagant use of fabric, including the voluminous sleeves. "Oh, look how rich I am, I even have ruffles of fabric which are utterly useless and cumbersome, (*gaffaw*)!"

During the 1440s, the houppelande shrank to knee-length. And got shorter still in the 1450s, barely covering the torso. Ooh err, missus! This was clearly a young man's fashion. The longer, more formal version was worn by the older men.

Alternatively, one may wear a **cotehardie**. It was a was a close-fitting garment worn over the doublet and hose, reaching the knee or mid-thigh. The cotehardie had long, slim sleeves. Again, a rich man thing, and was often made of silk or velvet.

The **doublet** was a long-sleeved, fitted garment with a front opening, made of wool or silk. It changed in the latter part of the 15th century; the waistline got lower and the chest became padded.

And don't forget those **hose**. Typically made of wool or linen, hose covered the feet and legs, and were tied to the doublet or braies (depending on what one was wearing). Towards the end of the 15th century, the two legs were more commonly sewn together to form one garment. Each leg could be made in a different colour, which was known as parti-colouring and may reflect the wearer's heraldic colours. But were almost always very tight (*coughs*).

With shorter styles, no wonder the **codpiece** was worn, otherwise one's proverbial family jewels would be on display! This was a pocket or pouch worn over the genitals. Cod being slang for scrotum btw.

In actual fact, in 1463, King Edward IV's parliament made it *compulsory* for a man to cover *"his privy Members and Buttokes"*. (*snickers*) Was there too much temptation, fellas?

Men's Headwear

The men also wore hats – everyone was expected to convey religious modesty.

The most humble of these was perhaps the **hood**. A simple cloth (wool in winter) which was loose at the back, and sometimes had a wrap-around, pointy tail (the liripipe). They had a little cape attached which sat about the shoulders. I should point out that hoods were worn by both men and women.

The **chaperon** was a type of hood. But the face opening was rolled up and worn atop the head. In the 15th century it had become a hat with a rounded brim which had a long taper (a liripipe or tippet) that was wound around and then left to hang down one side. The length of said liripipe is said to have even sometimes reached floor length. This was clearly another item for the rich to show off how much fabric they could afford to waste. They varied in style but can maybe be vaguely described as turban-esque.

In contrast, there was a **sugarloaf** hat which was stout and cylindrical. It could be made from felt, wool, taffeta or brocade. And could be trimmed with jewels or fur. It was this type of hat that King Richard III sported. A little bit like a fez.

The **bycocket** was still around. It could be worn by either sex, but we associate them more with men. Typically, felted and starched, with the wide brim turned up/pointed at one end. Think of the stereotypical Robin Hood hat.

Indeed, it was a hat worn by archers to keep the sun out of their eyes. And, if it was raining, turn it around to keep water off your neck. Because of this handy element, people wore them in the fields and whilst out hunting. It was pretty universally worn.

Another fine sun protection hat was the **straw** one. These had started to fall out of fashion in the 15th century, but workers still used them.

If in doubt, wear a **cap**. They were still around and could be made from pretty much any comfy material, so could be made to suit any budget. Usually worn over a coif.

Under their hats, they may have sported a bowl cut hairstyle and were clean shaven. But from maybe the mid-15th century, hair was starting to get longer, peeking out from under those hats and covering the ears.

Under Garments

Underneath one's outer garments, a man would wear an **undershirt or tunic** which was usually made of linen and could be as long as knee or even ankle length. Poor folk may have worn ones made of hemp cloth. This was often tucked into their underwear.

Knickers! Historians are very excited — some items have been found and dated to around the 15th century which to all intents and purposes are knickers. Along with these, are rudimentary linen garments in the form of bras, but without underwires or elastic support, obviously. So, these appear to have been for women.

What about men? Thanks to what are presumably hilarious drawings of men with their undergarments revealed, we do know they wore *something*.

And, in the Rule of St Benedict (written in the 6th century), there is a stipulation for monks who are sent on important errands outside the monastery to wear "drawers". It's fairly safe to assume that, when living in the flipping cold country that is England, the brethren wore these all winter too. They had precious few fires, and nobody wants to be a "brass monkey".

Towards the end of the medieval era, these became known as **braies**, and could vary in length and bagginess according to what one was wearing over them. No VPL, please!

If it helps, think of them as our modern boxer shorts. The hose would then be tied to the braies to hold them up.

In summary; layers! They all wore several layers.

Accessories

Let's accessorise!

Bags

All people carried **purses**. Yes, in 15th England, the man bag was just a purse like everyone else's (*fights the urge to quote Blackadder II because it would get me into copyright trouble*).

Purses were little bags, usually tied to the belt for carrying small items.

There was another type of small bag called a **poke**. I only really mention that as the 'little poke' which was worn *under* clothing later became a **pocket**.

More so in the 12th century, but there were also **scrips**. These were little shoulder bags used by pilgrims to carry items such as a repair kit or fire-starting equipment — the essentials for long journeys.

Wallets were larger, square purses, most commonly made of leather used for carrying food. And in the late medieval era, shoulder straps were added to be used as a sort of early messenger bag. But Paul in my book, *Love Habit*, uses one as a rudimentary first aid kit.

Belts

Special mention must be made of belts. I have alluded to their utilitarian usage already, but they really were there for a purpose. Eek, now I'm thinking of Batman!? But like him, the medieval folk did hang stuff off their belts, but more in the way of items such as:

- A coin purse
- Herbs (in a pouch)
- Keys
- A knife (cutting food usage) - everybody
- Paternoster (prayer beads)
- Tools
- Weapons

Belts were usually narrow, made of leather and worn low on the hip. But they could also be made of woven braid or wool.

Of course, rich ladies wore more jewelled or silk 'girdles'. Like everything else, how one's belt was decorated was a symbol of wealth and status.

Earrings

Earrings were rarely worn – hairstyles and/or hats covered the ears anyway. In the 13th century, the Church had actually banned the piercing of ears. That seems to have made the disreputable men folk wear them more — think thieves.

As hair and hat styles grew shorter and the ears were revealed, folk started to wear earrings again, particularly in the Tudor era.

Monk's Clothing

Look, you probably won't need this but information about habits is like hen's teeth, so I'm giving you what I gleaned so it's less of a nightmare should you find yourself desiring to know.

Their robes held deeply religious significance. The tunic represented the soul, whilst the hood was a reminder of their Vow of Obedience, and the outfit was plain to reflect their simple way of life and humility.

Right, so monks wore different colours according to their order (as discussed under 'Religion'). Those colours were subject to change, depending on their own house and/or region/climate. Even the actual garments may have varied also.

But, for Benedictine monks in the 15th century, they seem to have worn:

- **Postulant** – their own (probably colourful but more demure) clothing
- **Novice** – after a whole ceremony, they were issued a black tunic, scapula (like a tabard) and a hooded cloak
- **Junior Monk** – the hooded cloak was replaced by the cowl (hood), and cincture (official, corded belt); issued after taking Simple Vows

The **tonsure** (hair cut into a crown with a bald patch) was a renunciation of fashion and ego. It possibly was cut to emulate the Crown of Thorns of Christ. It was only cut once they had completed their novitiate and taken Simple Vows to become a Junior Monk.

Writing Prompt – Clothing

It's time to get dressed.

- What does your MC wear?
- Does someone have to help them get dressed?
- How long/short is their clothing?
- Is it brightly coloured?
- Are there jewels on their clothes?
- How long are the points on their shoes?
- Do they carry a bag?

KNIGHTS AND WEAPONRY

When one thinks of the Middle Ages, one may well imagine grand displays of knights jousting in tournaments. However, it rather depends on which section of this long era you look at.

Hm, this gets a bit complicated. And I'm going to state I'm not a weapons expert — I'm a lover not a fighter. This post aims to cover the basics.

So, knights first appeared around the 8th century, according to popular opinion.

However, the **Code of Chivalry**, although it may have been around in rudimentary forms even in Ancient Britain, was developed in the 11th-12th centuries. This was the code brought in to bring a sense of order to, let's face it, what had become thugs. To temper the fierce warrior with acts of valour — to bring a balance to the force, if you will (*wink wink*).

With this aim, they were taught things such as poetry; composing and performing. A knight was also instructed in good manners, including those whilst at table.

Chivalry is derived from the French word 'chevalier', and basically means 'one who rides and fights on a horse'.

Fun fact; between 1358-1488, there were 68 **women** appointed knights in England's Order of the Garter. Just in case you missed it when I mentioned this before. What? I'm impressed. It's worth repeating, *non*?

I discussed previously, how feudalism was in decline. The severely reduced population needed farmers to grow food. But our lands also needed to be defended. This little island we call home has had its fair share of invaders, after all.

Mercenaries were recruited in greater numbers — bought/hired soldiers as opposed to dedicated knights brought up and trained by nobles. Yes, these mercenaries were viewed as having dodgy allegiances and could not be entirely relied upon. I mean, by definition, they'd kind of work for the highest bidder.

When Henry VII returned to England to fight the Battle of Bosworth, he landed with 5,000-8,000 men. It's estimated that 1,800 of these were French mercenaries and formed the core of his army. Others were exiles. He then gathered recruits from the Welsh/English borders, including deserters from Richard III's army.

NB The title of "Sir" which came along with being a knight was *not* hereditary. One still had to train as a knight if you wanted that privilege.

Being a or having knights was costly. The price of the armour alone was high. One account says you could get really "cheap", probably ill-fitting armour for up to (the equivalent of) $30,000 (£22k). But, in the 15th century, a full suit of plate armour was more in the region of $500,00 - $3.5million. So, let's say, about £1million!!

HOWEVER, I'm going to add some confusion here. A **knight's full armour** is often quoted at around £16 in medieval money, which works out to be approx. £11,000. The Milanese, ready-made set may be around £8 (£5,500 in today's money).

I don't know why there are such wide variances in these estimations. The £11k region sounds much more realistic, given their status and income, though.

So, knights were very wealthy. And their fathers were probably knights too.

The cost of **training** was also high. It took many years. Let's look at the stages:

- ❖ **Page** = aged 7-10 up until 13 (horses, hunting, mock weapons)
- ❖ **Squire** = 14 to 18-21 (assistant to knight, weapons and armour, education, chivalry)
- ❖ **Dubbing** = 18-21 (made a knight)
- ❖ **Service** = from then on (guard for baron, fight in wars, tournaments)

In summary; there weren't that many actual knights in 15th century England. And they weren't likely to be seen cavorting around in tournaments. Sorry. I was disappointed too.

A lot of them had become more akin to landed gentry, lording it over estates and taking on roles such as Justice of the Peace.

Coat of Arms

I don't want to harp on too much about these as you probably won't need details on this. But know that nobles did indeed have a coat of arms which would be emblazoned on their knight's armour, banners etc.

And so, we must discuss **heraldry** — the symbols which made up said coat of arms. Let's just look at a few of the most common.

Colours again were important and symbolic:
- **Black** – wisdom, prudence, grief, constancy
- **Blue** (Azure) - unwavering loyalty, chastity, faith, truth and strength
- **Green** – loyalty in love relationships. Also: hope, joy and prosperity
- **Purple** – royalty, regal, sovereignty, justice
- **Red** – military strength (a cunning warrior), magnanimity
- **Silver / White** (Argent) - truth, innocence, purity, sincerity and peace
- **Yellow / Gold** – wisdom, constancy, faithfulness, glory, great generosity

Symbols

- **Battle Axe** - a military leader. Often associated with the Crusades.
- **Bear** - a fierce protector and a sign of great strength and/or healing
- **Chains** – a powerful alliance, or a mighty service/deed
- **Chessrook** - protection
- **Dog** – Loyalty (particularly to the monarch)
- **Dragon** – protection, great strength and faithfulness
- **Ducks** - successful and creative in business achievements (I know, not the most obvious animal to have)
- **Elephant** - great strength and devotion to duty
- **Falcon** – usually reserved for nobles
- **Flames** - zeal, rebirth, purification and even intense passion
- **Grapes** - good fortune, wealth/prosperity, luck
- **Hawthorne Tree** - intends bad luck to enemies of the arm's bearer. A form of magick protection / a ward.
- **Lion** - great courage, nobility and bravery, especially in battle

Certain shapes and placements also get involved, but that's getting too technical, I think.

Yes, I did design a coat of arms for Sir William in *Love in the Roses*. Did I mention what a geek I am? I'm proud to be one.

Right, so, Sir William's CoA has an azure field/background with a cross dancetty, with four chessrooks vert.

His core values are: chivalry, justice and protection, so I pretended his family's coat of arms represented those. Loyalty and truth are also strongly implied. Here's what it looks like:

Weapons

The **sword** is probably the most associated weapon with the knight. There was the long sword, about 60cm (1metre) long, for slashing.

The second option was a **falchion**, a single-edged sword which came to a point. It was light and shorter but with the power of an axe, ideal for close combat. Powerful blows could be dealt as well as effective slashing. However, the longer sword would deal the most powerful blows.

A **dagger** would also be worn, their last resort choice.

All that posturing at jousting tournaments wasn't just to get laid! The **lance** was used from horseback in battle too.

Plate armour posed a problem; it was tough to get through (hence the cost!). So, weapons advanced to counteract that. The **pollaxe**/poleaxe was used for this purpose, whilst on foot.

Spiked, flail weapons could be used whilst on foot too, but they were difficult to aim effectively with.

The **mace** was also a close combat option. A club-type, blunt weapon with a flange or knob on the end to pierce armour.

The **longbow** rose to prominence in the 13th century. About this time, laws were introduced in England, requiring every person to practice archery. Basically, the king wanted to be able to call upon *anyone* to go shoot his enemies. To be fair, it worked, as Henry V arguably won the **Battle of Agincourt in 1415** on the strength of his bowmen.

Archers made up 5/6ths of the army at that battle. Casualties: France 10,000 vs a few hundred for England.

This weapon also claims to have been the most decisive used in The Hundred Years War and The Wars of the Roses. It had a 200-metre range and could pierce armour at close range.

It was cheaper to use **archers**. But the men-at-arms and knights were very useful in protecting those archers. Incidentally, some archers were also wealthy and wore good armour.

Armour

Knights primarily wore plate armour in 15th century England.

It was articulated, meaning one could move freely. And was lighter than perhaps one would expect.

Again, layers! It would take around 25 minutes to put a full suit of armour on.

Braies and hose would be worn, and an **arming jacket**; a padded coat/jacket.

A coif would be a barrier between the hair and helmet.

Greaves; leg armour would cover the legs and calves, tied on with leather straps. A **cuisse** would protect the upper leg, thighs and knees – also helped protect the groin. Tied at the top with points to the arming jacket. The back would not be plated, to enable comfortable horse riding.

A **maille skirt** then went on as a sort of belt; the main protection for the groin and points and where other armour attaches.

Should one not have been using a squire, one certainly would be required from here.

The **breast plate** got put on, which covered the chest and ribs. It went on from the side as there was a hinged section for the front and back. The **plackart** then went over the top of this to cover the lower torso. All fastened with side buckles. **Tassets** hung down from here to protect the upper thighs whilst mounted on a horse.

Next was the arm layers; the **vambrace**. They were in several pieces tied together with straps. The **lower cannon** was the part for the lower arm. **The guard of vambrace** was the section covering the elbow/inner arm on the rein-bearing side. On the other arm, the **couter** (elbow piece) was smaller cut away to allow for the use of a lance.

Large **pauldrons** protected the shoulders and heart in a double layer. Again, smaller on the lance-bearing side. You could attach a lance rest to the breast plate for a lance's grapper to hook onto.

The **bevor** was then donned to protect the throat and neck. It had a part which could be raised to cover the lower part of the face.

A helmet, preferably with a visor (but not always) would get plonked onto one's head. The visor did limit vision but would offer better protection from missile weapons.

And finally, the gauntlets (gloves).

Men-At-Arms

After the Battle of Agincourt, we kinda realised that cavalry charges against archers were futile. England now used more men-at-arms. They wore plate armour and rode to battle but now *mostly* fought on foot.

A man-at-arms *could* be a knight, but he might also be a retainer or mercenary — served through feudal obligation or for pay. Although, they were paid half as much as knights, their armour was paid for by their lord or king. These chaps might be anyone with arms training. Technically, he was a fully-armoured heavy cavalryman.

Knights were viewed as being of a higher social class. But had to pay for their own armour, equipment and horses.

When fighting on horseback, a man-at-arms was probably using a **demi-lance** as his main weapon in the 15th century. On foot, they may have cut down their lance down to 5ft, or used a two-handed poleaxe.

'Comme Nostre Frere' - Knightly Ritual Brotherhood

Um, so there were ceremonies which were incredibly similar to marriage, where two men may commit themselves to one another in a holy space. In theory, this was to ensure a bonding of brotherhood, particularly those about to go off and fight.

In essence, it was a legal undertaking in which ritual brothers became the heirs to each other's martial fortunes, shared their spoils and paid one another's ransoms.

However, no conditions seem to have been imposed. Instead, they maybe willingly chose to honour certain obligations because of their mutual love. But was that love romantic or borne out of close friendship?

It appears to be similar to *adelphopoiesis*, which was "brother-making" thought to have originated between monks in around the 4th century. It was **a union of two people of the same sex, usually men, recognised by the church.**

Both unions have sparked much debate amongst historians, as you can imagine. One doesn't tend to undergo such a ritual for friends. But perhaps when facing almost certain death, maybe you would.

Oh, come on, this was gay marriage! Wasn't it?

Wars of 15th Century England

I'm not a fan of war, obviously. However, when we look at lists of wars/battles, we get a sense of what the populace was concerned about e.g. religion, territory, trade routes etc. So, they can be useful to give us context.

- **Hundred Years War** - 10th November 1337 to 17th July 1453 – England & Burgundy vs France & Scotland – The French won. England lost everything in France except Calais, but as most of the fighting happened on French soil, the English may have come back with some plunder.
- **(Battle of Agincourt, during the Hundred Years War)** – 25th October 1415 – England won and dominated the war until...
- **(Siege of Orléans, during the Hundred Years War)** – 12th October 1428 to 8th May 1429 – Joan of Arc led France to victory
- **(The Battle of Castillon, during the Hundred Years War)** – 17th July 1453 – viewed as the final battle of the war, France won. Notable also for the first time that field artillery (canons) played a major role.

- **Owain Glyndwr's Rebellion** (Welsh Revolt) - Autumn 1400 to Autumn 1415 – Wales vs England – England won
- **The Wars of the Roses** - 22nd May 1455 to 16th June 1487 – England vs England; House of York against House of Lancaster (who were all technically Plantagenets) – Lancaster sort of won, but established the House of Tudor
- **The Italian War** - October 1494 to 7th April 1498 – France vs the League of Venice (Venice, Naples, Papal States, Spain, Milan, Florence, England) – but England didn't have much involvement tbh, but English mercenaries were in high demand.

Wars of the Roses (Key Battles)
- **The Battle of St Albans** (22 May 1455) - a Yorkist victory, and Richard, Duke of York was declared Protector (later overturned)
- **The Battle of Northampton** (10 July 1460) - another Yorkist victory, and Henry VI was captured. The queen fled to Wales.
- **The Battle of Wakefield** (30 December 1460) - a Lancastrian victory. Richard, Duke of York killed. Succeeded by Edward, his son.
- **The Battle of Towton** (29 March 1461) - the Earl of Warwick led the Yorkists to victory; King Henry, Queen Margaret and the Prince of Wales flee to Scotland. Possibly the bloodiest battle ever fought on British soil; estimated 28,000 fatalities!
- **The Battle of Tewkesbury** (04 May 1471) - the Yorkists were victorious. Prince of Wales killed and the queen captured.
- <u>**The Battle of Bosworth Field**</u> (22 August 1485) - King Richard III killed. Henry VII crowned
- **The Battle of Stoke Field** (16 June 1487) - Yorkist commanders killed. Tudor reign stabilised.

Above, I've listed the key battles of the Cousins War (Wars of the Roses as we name it today). It's interesting as the battles were relatively few and far between. But much happened in between too. There were princes placed into custody and subsequently went missing. Kings and queens were captured, monarchs fled, others came back to fight. The Crown changed hands six times. Oh, such turmoil!

The Yorkist and Lancastrian supporters weren't clearly defined by geographical boundaries, but it's fair to say that there were more Yorkist supporters in the north, funnily enough, using York as a base.

Lancastrians seemed to congregate in Wales as well as the obvious Lancashire region. If you look at a map of loyalties, House Lancaster holds the widest spread, reaching far down the south of England.

You could find supporters for either house in most places if you looked hard enough, though.

Writing Prompt – Knights

Fight, fight, fight! But who's involved?

- Is your MC a lover or a fighter?
- Are they a knight? Or do they hold dominion over such?
- Do they have any cool weapons?
- How long do they spend at weapons practice?
- (*gasp*) Are they in a battle?

TRANSPORT / TRAVEL

Can we please just take a moment to admire this drawing of a pony? I'm a poor artist, but this looks convincingly like a horse! Right, sorry, where were we?

Alrighty, let us turn our attention to transport. How do your characters get about?

Roads were terrible — dirt tracks which would get absolutely sodden in wet weather. They were also often overrun with bandits.

The common man didn't have much need of travel. There may be servants going to market for their masters. But other than that, the roads were reserved for the merchants, pedlars, pilgrims, messengers, armies and the wealthy going between homes. Rich pickings for those bandits!

There were, of course, pedestrians. Going by foot was common for the pilgrims, for example.

However, the most common form of transport was the horse.

Types of Horse

The **destrier** was the crème de la crème of the horses. It was a warhorse, renowned for its supreme strength. Used also in jousting tournaments. However, endurance was not their best quality. They were certainly imposing, standing at around 15 hands, and were well-muscled. The destrier was rare and incredibly expensive.

So, the **courser** (or charger) was more commonly found in use by knights and men-at-arms. They had a slighter, shorter build, but maintained speed and strength.

I'm including the **lyard**. But it's not really a horse *type*, to be honest. But I'm rather partial to a dapple grey, and that's what these were. Incidentally, **favelle** was the medieval name for a chestnut (brown) horse, and **bayard** was what we now call a bay (reddish brown with black points).

With a lighter weight than the coursers, mild manner and a smooth gait, the **palfrey** was a highly sought after riding, trotting horse. They could amble over long distances. So, naturally, they were expensive. Mostly ridden by knights or noble ladies.

Jennets, seem to cause contradictory opinions. Some say the name was interchangeable with palfrey, whilst others regard jennets as slightly less desirable than them. Let's just say they were similar.

Rounceys were an everyday horse. The least expensive of these types. Fast and agile, they could still be seen ridden into battle or used as pack horses.

Then you had **draft** horses (aka affers or stotts) for pulling ploughs and heavy loads. They started to replace the ox. Large and muscly! Imagine the Budweiser Clydesdales (other brewery horses are not available but other Clydesdales are).

Workhorses as a type covers pack horses (aka sumpters) and cart horses. The shorter, stockier breeds.

NB These were all shorter than the horses we see today. They would be considered small riding horses now. The shorter types were more akin to our ponies.

Also, all those heavy horses' hooves in mud? Yeah, those road conditions could only get worse. As someone who's ridden through such conditions, it gets pretty dicey, let me tell you!

Saddles

The saddles had a high front and back; the cantle wrapped around the rider — comfy and secure. Well, yes, until your horse fell - oops! Yeah, you could be crushed to death. The inability to twist may have caused life-threatening internal damage too. Jumping obstacles would have been incredibly difficult, as one needs to lean forwards in order to do so.

And whilst we're talking saddles, **ladies were more likely to sit astride**. The first true, single-rider, side-saddle in England seems to have appeared in the 16th century. Women would, however, sit to the side if they were mounted behind men.

Thinking about that confining saddle, when a lady became heavy with child, it was somewhat unusable. Yes, she could sit behind her husband. But the option of a litter was there. Although, these were most frequently used by the frail and elderly.

A **litter** was a sort of wheelless carriage on two wooden poles, carried between two horses (forward and aft). More of an open box, like a smaller version of the top of a cart. However, some litters do seem to have been enclosed; more like a sedan chair in appearance. I don't wish to confuse you, though — the sedan chair wasn't used in England until the 17th century.

Wheeled Conveyances

Covered wagons were around, but do not seem to have been popular. Well, the wheels could easily become stuck, and they halved the distance to around 20 miles per day. Nor were they comfy - the lack of spring-loaded suspension would have made the ride incredibly bumpy. And they were very expensive.

Carts were more appropriate for conveying goods than people.

By the way, if you had oxen pulling your cart, the distance would be halved again to 10 miles per day!

Our wondrous canal system had yet to be built. You could maybe get a **barge** on the River Thames, but that's not much good to the rest of the country.

And sea voyages were mainly for explorers, trade and war purposes.

Speed

So, how far and fast did they go?

A horses' walking pace is around 3-5mph. They could travel **up to around 40 miles per day**.

Horses trot at a speed of around 8mph, canter 15mph and gallop 30mph.

But these take energy and are not sustainable for extensive periods. You're looking at about 2-3 miles at a gallop, tops. Plus, the terrible road conditions wouldn't allow much more than a walk most of the time.

Fun fact: People walk around 3mph — so, about the same as a horse, weirdly.

So, when looking at how far my character, Isabel, travelled in a day, I looked at the old A-roads (obviously not motorways). And calculated the **walking time** on GoogleMaps. I did also reference old maps of the UK to check road routes.

Inns

When travelling, people probably needed to stay overnight somewhere.

Inns have been in existence for a very long time. But, as travel increased during the 14th century, so too did the number of inns. Prior to this, they were more of the tavern variety. Taverns were still around as a cheaper option but were rowdier – think more of a place to get drunk and sleep off the effects in a room out the back on a bed of straw.

Inns sought to accommodate the traveller with their horses (in stables) and wares. As such, they attracted the wealthier type of traveller.

Small towns and villages usually had one inn, but market towns typically had two to five, and cities may have had ten to twenty of them. They were desirable businesses to run as they could make a tidy profit (*bursts into the song from Les Misérables*).

Generally, one may find some form of lodging, or at least refreshment every 15 miles or so.

The bedchambers may have been private or house a few beds which several people (strangers) could share. Eww!

I'm going to refer to the Great Bed of Ware here, although it wasn't built until around 1590 (too late for our medieval folk). The White Hart Inn, Ware, was famous for this large bed which could accommodate up to four couples — that's eight people! I just find it amusing, so thought I'd share. Just why would you? Anyway...

Most large beds in inns slept 3-4 people. There may be a room containing 12 of these beds. Eurgh!

A dining room, somewhere to pray and a common area would also be provided.

The innkeeper may be involved in trade himself and was often quite a wealthy personage of good standing. I say he; only about 10% of innkeepers were women, likely widowed.

There was alternative accommodation — one could opt to overnight in the guest house of a monastery.

Writing Prompt –Transport

There's an important event, and your MC's been invited.

- How does your MC get there?
- How long does it take?
- Where do they lay their head to rest?

PASTIMES

It wasn't all work and no play.

How did the wealthy spend their time? Well, managing their estates did actually take a lot of their attention. And one was expected to undertake religious obligations too, mainly so as to avoid time in purgatory.

But once all their duties were complete, there was some time for leisure.

Play time!!!

Ladies often undertook **needlework**/embroidery. Again, this also had a practical application as they could decorate wall or bed hangings with their creations.

Dancing (and drinking) happened rather a lot. Well, there were many saints' days to celebrate (*shrugs*).

Touring monks may perform religious **plays**. And travelling **entertainers** would enact plays, recite poems, play music, tumble (performed acrobatics), juggle and sing songs.

Games

Gambling was popular, usually around games of dice or cards.

Board games were played, especially at Christmastide:
- **Tables** (an early form of backgammon)
- **Halatafl** (originally, a Viking game aka Fox & Geese)
- **Queek** (betting on how many stones would land on black/white squares of a chequered board/cloth)
- **Chess**
- **Draughts** (checkers)
- **Raffle** (gambling on three dice rolling the same number)
- **Nine Men's Morris** (aka Merrills)
- **Shove-board** – weighted discs shoved down a long table
- **Shove ha'penny** (previously known as Shove Groat) – a smaller version of shove-board for commoners, especially in taverns

Other options were:

- **Ring toss** – small rings were aimed at small stakes in the ground; similar to quoits
- **Knucklebones** was very much like modern jacks but using actual sheep's knucklebones (*heave*)
- Or why not play a rousing game of **skittles** (similar to ten pin bowling)
- **Bobbing for apples** is always amusing, right? Our forefathers enjoyed it just as much as us. Especially around All Saints Day (aka *Alholowmesse*)
- **Snap Apple** was a hilarious version – a plank of wood was suspended from a ceiling; from one end hung an apple, and a lit candle from the other. Whilst it spun, folk would try to bite the apple. (*hollers for health & safety!*)

Children's Games

But won't somebody please think of the children? LOL. Yes, they had fun too.

There is evidence of people using **stilts** and playing **hoops** (rolled with a stick). And **marbles** were fired at one another.

Hobby horses were ridden. Sometimes the pole would not even be adorned with the representation of a horse's head! There were also ceramic animal **figurines**.

Wooden **spinning tops** were popular as they could be made at home. **Dolls**, were likewise readily supplied. They may even had miniature dining sets made of crockery for said dolls.

Even **tag, tug-of-war, leapfrog and hide and seek** seem to have been enjoyed. And there are many depictions of **snowball fights**.

Rattles were certainly given to children. Funny how some things stand the test of time, eh?

Sport

Sport covered a multitude of activities.

Jousting and tournaments did happen sometimes. A knight had to be able to show off, after all. The more dangerous the better (*eyeroll*)! Lances, swords and the bow would be included in such events. However, during the 15th century, these were **not** very common, so please use with caution.

Archery practice was mandatory as well as a sport, bear in mind. So, anyone and everyone had access to this. Quite useful in times of trouble! But they could have competitions or tournaments of such, even the women. This may have happened particularly around festivities such as Whitsun, after Mass, of course.

A rudimentary version of **football** was played, especially around Eastertide. A pig's bladder would be kicked across a designated area of the village/town. The use of hands seems to have been allowed. I gather this could get rather rowdy and injuries were not uncommon. In fact, one of the few rules was for it 'not to lead to manslaughter'.

The men folk could enjoy some manly **wrestling** if they were so inclined.

Stoolball (similar to rounders or baseball) was in existence. I grew up in a town where this was still played! The bat had a small, round, paddled head.

Hunting comes under the heading of sport, I'm afraid. The nobles hunted on horseback with dogs, often for deer.

Or with birds - **falconry** was huge. One should not be seen in public without one's hawk upon their wrist, wot wot.

The female falcon was bigger and fiercer than the male hawk, so was the most prized. They could catch all manner of unassuming creatures, such as cranes, ducks, geese, herons, pheasants or even hares.

However, they do moult once per year (between May-August), which puts them out of service for a while.

Men, women, old and young could enjoy hawking, thanks to its more sedate pace. It was also deemed safer.

In fairness, any quarry was probably enjoyed at dinner.

I'm sorry, but they did also have **animal fights**. Cocks, dogs, bulls, bears and even lions were pitted against one another, with gambling heavily involved (*shudder*).

Music

Let's focus on something far more pleasant, shall we?

When thinking of medieval music, there were two main kinds

- ❖ Religious
- ❖ Celebratory

Chants (Religious)

In churches, one would have been immersed in the haunting sound of Gregorian Chant — the religious singing of Psalms in a monophonic style (one melodic line). Some examples of specific chants:

- *Phos Hilaron* (O Gladsome Light) may have been sung as the lamps were lit at vespers.
- Also at vespers, for the Feast of St John the Baptist; *Ut Queant Laxis* (So That They May Be Free)
- *Iam vere scimus* (Now We Really Know) – sung at Christmas
- *Puer natus in Bethlehem* (A child is born in Bethlehem) – for the Nativity
- *Simeon, Nunc Dimittis* (The Canticle of Simeon) – sung at Candlemas
- *Gaude Maria Virgo*, in honour of the Blessed Virgin Mary – also for Candlemas
- *Ave Rex Noster* (Hail our King) – on Palm Sunday
- *Christus resurgens* (Christ is risen) – sung on Easter Sunday

Everyday Music

But music also played a vital part of entertainment. The big houses would either employ the travelling players/minstrels or have their own musicians. Minstrels would recite poetry of heroism and romance to the accompaniment of a harp. Mimes and more instruments were added through the Middle Ages. They also sang fabliaux; humorous, grotesque stories.

They would serenade the dishes into feasts. And, after dinner, these minstrels would play the music for dancing.

Musical instruments included:

- Bagpipes
- Cittern (a bit like a mandolin)
- Cornett (more like a pipe)
- Cymbals
- Dulcimer (string instrument plucked with hammers)
- Drums (kettle and snare/tabor)
- Flageolet (similar to a recorder)
- Flute
- Gitterm (from 13th century, similar to a lute)
- Hand-bells
- Harp
- Harpsichord
- Hurdy gurdy (a lovely name! A crank and string operated instrument)
- Lute (from 15th century and very popular)
- Pipe (3 holed, could be played with one hand)
- Pipe organs (in churches)
- Recorder
- Sackbut (another glorious name! Predecessor to the trombone)
- Shawm (predecessor to the oboe)
- Timbrel (tambourine)
- Trumpet (more like horns)
- Viol (late medieval, predecessor to the cello)
- Violin

Dance

I think humans have danced ever since we popped onto this mortal coil. But, in the 15th century, they had two main types of dance.

Country Dancing

These were often performed in lines and involved clapping and spinning e.g. *farandole*.

Circle dances such as carol/e and estampie were also part of the country dance repertoire.

Also around were the *colonese, pizochara* and *chirintana*.

Court Dancing

This was more reserved/refined and included things such as *bassedanse* (there are variations of spelling) — processional dances where the feet did not leave the ground e.g. *pavane*.

The *galliard* was an athletic dance, containing leaps, jumps and hops. In particular, there was a large jump, after which the dancer lands with one leg ahead of the other.

However, there are later dance manuals showing the haute dance which had leaps and lifts.

Because there is little documentary evidence of these, there are contradictory definitions for these forms and when/where they were used. I reckon the posh folk still jumped about a bit. But you can be pretty sure the peasants got loud and lively with theirs as it was usually associated with outdoor celebrations such as the harvest.

One dance we do know was around from the 14th century is the *saltarello*. Its name comes from the Italian *saltare* – to jump. Italy was also its country of origin. It was usually performed in a triple meter (fast). A double step with a hop was its main highlight.

Go on, have a jig. Shake your groove thing!

Writing Prompt – Pastimes

- What does you MC do for fun?

Yes, that's all I'm going to ask on this one. Let your imagination run wild.

INSULTS / SLANG

I've saved the best for last! Something that most people want to know sooner or later is swear words. And as writers, we must allow our characters a little expletive from time to time. Sometimes, you just gotta call people names when they upset you, or cry out when injured.

Swearing has changed a lot over the years – words which are innocuous now were once cause for fisticuffs or even suing. Remember, in medieval England, a woman could sue another for being called a whore. Men thought it the most heinous insult in the world to be called a fool and could come to blows if thus affronted.

'A turd in your teeth' was a common insult back in the 15th century - it's so awesome I had to include it in my book, *Love in the Roses*. Akin to 'eat shit'.

'**Fopdoodle**' is perhaps my favourite medieval insult, meaning a stupid person, but in a friendly way, like we'd say, "You eedyut." I've made it my mission to try to re-introduce it in today's society. Try using it in a sentence today.

'Alackaday' was a fab exclamation. A contraction of alack the day; used to express sorrow or dissatisfaction.

And yes, I included a lengthy glossary in my novels to provide meanings for words and terms no longer in common use.

Insults

During the medieval era, insults could be really quite inventive. Several words may be strung together to create one grand tirade of hatred.

There were a few different categories to target:

- ❖ Cleanliness
- ❖ Intelligence
- ❖ Manners
- ❖ Profession
- ❖ Social status

Add in some sort of animal reference, and you're onto a witty winner!

So, let's look at some specific words:

- ❖ **Avaunt** – begone/away
- ❖ **Bawdy** - lewd person
- ❖ **Bellicose** - inclined to fighting
- ❖ **Bitch** – derogatory term used against a woman
- ❖ **Caitiff** - a contemptible or cowardly person
- ❖ **Churl/ish** - without manners/of low birth
- ❖ **Corpulent** - stout, fat
- ❖ **Cumberworld** - someone who is an encumbrance on the world; a useless person or thing; from Middle English combre-world
- ❖ **Dalcop** - literally a "dull-head", a particularly stupid person
- ❖ **Decrepit** - broken down in health, weakened, especially by age; mid-15th century
- ❖ **Drate-poke** - someone who mumbles/speaks indistinctly
- ❖ **Droning** - monotonous tone
- ❖ **Fie** – a general exclamation of annoyance

- **Fool** – stupid person; caution - deeply insulting
- **Fopdoodle** - a stupid person
- **Fusty** - stale-smelling
- **Fuzzle** - to make drunk, to confuse or befuddle
- **Gallows-gift** - dangerous criminal
- **Hedge-born** – lowest class of person
- **Irksome** - annoying, troublesome
- **Jape** - say or do something in jest or mockery
- **Knave** - rogue/rascal
- **Lascivious** -lustful, inclined to lust
- **Leasing-monger** - liar
- **Pizzle** - penis of a bull used as a flogger
- **Pox-ridden** - diseased
- **Prattle** - foolish, inconsequential talk
- **Prating fool** – is therefore a fool who talks too much
- **Rascal** – dishonest person of the lowest class
- **Quake-buttock quaffer** - a trembling, heavy drinker
- **Sot** – a drunkard
- **Spleenful** - ill-humored, irritable or peevish, spiteful - the spleen being the seat of ill-temper
- **Tardy** - slow, late, stupid
- **Timorous** – fearful
- **Wattle** – foolish talk
- **Varlet** - an insult based on social class, a dishonest man, a rascal (from valet)
- **Wastrel** - a good-for-nothing
- **Wellaway** – a cry of dismay akin to 'oh, dear me' - literally "woe, lo, woe!"
- **Wench** - a whore/strumpet
- **Winebibber** - habitual drinker/drunkard
- **Wretch** - vile, despicable person
- **Yaldson** - son of a prostitute

Try combining a couple of these, you pox-ridden, fuzzle-headed, wastrel! No, wait, come back, I didn't mean it. I love you, really xx

NB If you do look up other insults online, do double-check their etymology; a lot of sites claim to list medieval insults, but are more Shakesperean or even Victorian.

Drunk as in had too much alcohol was a term. But one could say politely that someone was, "in their cups".

A useful phrase on its own is "beshrew thee (you)" – the original f off! In its literal sense, it means 'curse you'. Similar to "fie thee" – fie expresses disgust or outrage.

Speaking of, **the 'f word'**, it was **not** yet in use. Sorry. I was disappointed too. The etymology is tricky. It seems to have Germanic origins, and initially meant 'to strike'.

It was supposedly a surname in 13th century: Carl Buck's, 1949 *Dictionary of Selected Synonyms in the Principal Indo-European Languages,* references John le Fucker from the year 1278. But this is dubious, however fun.

Interestingly, there is a manuscript of *De Officiis*, in which an anonymous monk made a note in the margin, "**O d fuckin Abbot**." He dated another note in that same text, 1528 – too late for us medieval writers. Incidentally, the 'd' likely stands for 'damned' which clearly was too heinous to write in full, but 'fuck' was alright by him. LOL. But he does seem to mean it in a sexually derisive way.

Instead, one can use **sard** or **swive**. e.g. "Don't sard another man's wife."

Or, if you're desperately trying to beg forgiveness (alternatively, if you're being tickled beyond standing; looks at Paul in *Love Habit*) – "I cry mercy".

Euphemisms for Private Parts

I really struggled to find helpful words for one's bits. And, especially writing *Love Habit*, I needed several. Cock is such a great word, as is dick – neither are 15th century appropriate, however. Even phallus, which I had assumed was ancient, seems to only date back to 1610! So, here's what I found that one could use.

- **Ballocks** – (spelled with an 'a' not an 'o'), testicles; from Old English *bealluca* 'to blow, swell'
- **Balls** - Meaning 'testicle' actually dates from early 14th century (knowing it comes from ballocks makes it make sense)
- **Belle-chose** – literally 'beautiful thing', vagina; used by Chaucer but also a medical text
- **Buttocks** - posterior/arse/bottom; c. 1300
- **Copulation** – joining/uniting; late 14th century, from Latin *copulationem*.
- **Cunt** – vagina; not deemed vulgar, and even appeared in medical texts in 1220
- **I will have esement** – a phrase for a man desiring sexual release (guy needs to cum!)
- **Nether** – general term for any genitalia - down, below, beneath; Old English. In Middle English (and after) used also of body parts.
- **Pillicock** – penis; early 14th century
- **Pintel** – penis, specifically human; Old English but of unknown origin
- **Pizzle** - penis of a bull used as a flogger
- **Prick** – 'to have sex with a woman' was used by Chaucer in the late 14th century, but not as a penis until Shakespeare in 1590
- **Sard** – old form of the 'f word'
- **Self-pollution** - discharge of semen other than during sex (wanking)

- **Spitter** – very slang term for penis
- **Stif bourdon** – an erection; again, used by Chaucer
- **Swive** – a really negative way of saying have sex with; Chaucer
- **Taketh hym by the hand and hard hym twiste** – Old English way of saying you gave him a wank
- **Tarse** - penis; Old English, pre-1150
- **Testicle** - early 15th century, alteration of testicule (late 14th century), from Latin *testiculus*
- **Tewel** – anus or rectum; used by Chaucer in 14th century

Now, I don't want to cast shade, but a lot of these do seem to be dated back to Chaucer. He was a very naughty author! Also, apologies, but female genitalia didn't come up in my research much.

By the way, if someone wishes to go to the loo/toilet, "going to siege" was a euphemism for that.

Talking of toilets again (I promise I'm not obsessed!), but on the above list, "I will have esement," means needing to ejaculate. However, when we were looking at public toilets, they had the nickname of, "house of easement'. Does this infer public lavs have always been a bit seedy and a place for lustful activity? Or is it just two meanings of the same word? Hmm (*ponders*).

Anyway…

Compliments

Let's end on a pleasant note by looking at ways of being nice.

"God give you good morning," was a pleasant greeting.

"By my troth," inferred a solemn vow/promise.

"Prythee" (spelled prithee from c. 1560) – a formal 'please', a contraction of 'pray thee'.

- **Comely** - used for a beautiful man or woman
- **Culver** - dove (or pigeon)
- **Dear heart** / my heart
- **Fairest of fair** - beautiful
- **Honey** / my honey swete - a term of endearment used even in the Bible!
- **Lief** - (sounds like leaf) - Middle English; beloved, dear
- **My best beloved** - most cherished
- **My darling** / my dear one
- **My heart's gleam** / root
- **My peerless paramour** - darling/sweetheart without equal; the best
- **My sweeting** - darling

Aaw! And upon this final entry, I bid you a fond farewell and wish you a good day.

Writing Prompt – Swearing

I beg your pardon. Did your MC just swear at me? LOL

- How polite are they?
- What do they call their 'bits'? Look, some things are important!
- Do they use any terms of endearment?

FAVOURITE RESOURCES

This is clearly *not* an academic book, and if I cited all of the sources I used to gain all this lovely information we'd be here all day. Plus, I'm not sure what they all were, I'll be honest – so much checking and double-checking happened.

So, instead, please permit me to share just some of my favourite treasure troves.

Podcasts

Indeed, I listened to many podcasts, especially when my hands were busy typing other things. The best ones I found were:

Betwixt The Sheets – A fab, fun, adulty podcast about adulty things. Dr Kate Lister is the saucy host of all things historical and sultry, usually joined by a subject matter expert. Available from wherever you usually get your podcasts e.g. BBC Sounds or Apple.

Gone Medieval – Pretty much anything you want to know about the medieval era, you will find it here. There are over 400 episodes! Matt Lewis and Dr. Eleanor Janega are the main hosts.

Websites

So many websites! Some are better informed than others. It's always a good idea to check more than one webpage tbh; verify the article is accurate. Sites such as Wikipedia are good, but as anyone can put anything on there, I'd recommend using caution.

www.medievalists.net - Definitely one of the best sites I found. Not only do they have a plethora of excellent articles, but they also suggest books to read and run online courses. AND they have podcasts. Simply marvellous!

www.worldhistory.org - Is another great resource. It includes an encyclopaedia, podcast, bookshop (& a shop for merch).

www.historyextra.com – Would be my third choice. It's the official website for BBC History Magazine - you can search under era nicely.

To be honest, you possibly don't need to look much further than those. Anything more specific will come up with an internet search.

However, there is one more site I'd recommend to you:

www.etymonline.com - To look up the etymology of some words, I suggest looking here. They will give you the word's meaning, first use and roots. Great for things you want to use often or for swearing etc. – the ones you scatter in as cant to give a flavour of the era.

YouTube

Alright, sometimes you just want to *watch* something fun and educational.

@ModernKnight – Is just one such YouTuber. Jason Kingsley CBE is the guy on there. He was formerly known for being the co-founder and CEO of video game developer Rebellion Developments, but now he dresses up in medieval garb and frolics on his magnificent horses. But don't let that fool you; the content is historically researched.

@TastingHistory – If you enjoy food, Max Miller creates recipes from history, and is fun to watch.

You can also find many medieval instrumental playlists on there to have on in the background whilst typing. I find this helpful, maybe you will too.

And, a wonderful TV series to watch is *Cadfael*. A lot of the details are surprisingly accurate. Set in 12th century northern England. It gives fab medieval vibes.

Books

How do I narrow this down?? I've read so many.

- **How to Behave Badly in Renaissance Britain** by Ruth Goodman is fun.
- **Life in a Medieval Castle** by Frances and Joseph Gies is informative.
- **Terry Jones' Medieval Lives** blends his Pythonic wit with useful information.
- **Life in the Medieval Cloister** by Julie Kerr is amazing. I wish I'd read it before I fished around a multitude of other places. Obviously, only good if you're writing about medieval monks. My fictional *Love Habit* is maybe a resource in its own right along those lines.
- **The Medieval Cookbook** by Maggie Black is a yummy resource for recipes, which notes the seasons/occasions for each dish, along with modern measurements so you can have a go yourself.
- But if you need monastery specific food, **Flans and Wine** by Brother William is handy.
- **Old English Medical Remedies** by Sinead Spearing is a good start for medicine.

Look, books tend to be about one very specific topic/area and are often very dry and academic. That's exactly why I wrote this one. Because I desperately wanted a one-stop-shop to start me off. I've written the book I needed.

Thank You

Thank you for reading *An Author's Research Notes on Medieval England*.

I hope you've found it both enjoyable and informative. Indeed, if you have, please do leave a review. I honestly appreciate each and every one. And reviews help other readers make an informed decision.

If I've intrigued you, one can **sign up for my newsletter by scanning the nifty QR code below,** to ensure you don't miss any exciting news (about new releases and/or special offers). It's also a great way of ensuring we don't lose contact should social media suddenly disappear.

And as a thank you gift, you can **claim your FREE exclusive copy of *Recipes From Love Habit*** when you sign up (routed via ProlificWorks) (at time of publishing).

If you would like to follow me on SM, @tlclarkauthor will usually find me. I am most frequently found lurking on **Instagram** or **TikTok**.

Did you know you can also follow authors on Amazon and therefore receive notifications when a new book is released?

But I am also present on **Goodreads** and **BookBub**, where I review the books I read; I'm eclectic.

Other Books by TL Clark

Non-Fiction

How To Write A Historical Novel And Love It

– A Beginner's Guide to Researching, Writing and Publishing a Historical Book

Historical Romance Fiction

Love Habit

– Paul expected to live a devout, chaste life as he entered the monastery. Until he met Luke. Set in 15th-century Kent, England.

Love in the Roses

– Isabel is the daughter of a knight and is about to marry a man she's never met.

Also set in 15th-century Kent, England.

Regency Love

– Discover what Lady Anne really thinks as she enters the marriage mart in 1814

A Haverton Christmas – A short story spin-off of Regency Love. Lady Caroline returns empty-handed from the Season, and her Christmas looks bleak.

Miss Georgiana Darcy's Quest For Love – A Pride & Prejudice variation novelette. Discover what happened to Georgiana after her dealings with Mr Wickham.

But should you wish to diversify your reading, her other titles include:

Other Romance Fiction

The Darkness & Light Duology - (Love Bites and Love Bites Harder) – In case you've not read it yet; this is my award-winning paranormal romance (m/f)

Love Bites MORE – The stand-alone follow-up; a m/m/m fated mates fantasy

Young's Love – a contemporary romance including gelato in Tuscany as Samantha strives for independence

True's Love – romantic suspense; Amanda finds more than cheap thrills in Ibiza

Dark Love – explore the love in a BDSM relationship and beyond with male submissive, Jonathan

Broken & Damaged Love – Tina comes to terms with her childhood abuse as she learns to love and trust again (there is a gay side character)

Rekindled Love – Join Sophie on her rollercoaster ride through life, from first to last love

Self Love – Molly goes on a quest to change her perspective on life and even herself

Love Gaia – A cli-fi romance set mainly in an underground in New Zealand as nuclear war breaks out

About the Author

TL Clark is an award-winning, best-selling, British author of love who stumbles through life as if it were a gauntlet of catastrophes.
Rather than playing the victim, she uses these unfortunate events to fuel her passion for writing, for reaching out to help others.
Her dream is to buy a farmhouse, so she can run a retreat for those who are feeling frazzled by the stresses of the modern world.
She writes about different kinds of love in the hope that she'll uncover its mysteries.

Her loving husband (and mourned-for cat) have proven to her that true love really does exist.
Writing has shown her that coffee may well be the source of life.

And she really hopes you found this book helpful yet fun.

www.ingramcontent.com/pod-product-compliance
Lightning Source LLC
Chambersburg PA
CBHW050337010526
44119CB00049B/576